Tune Up your Turnout

A Dancer's Guide

THE BODY SERIES

Tune Up your Turnout

A Dancer's Guide

Deborah Vogel

White Owl Publishing
Oberlin, Ohio

Tune Up Your Turnout: A Dancer's Guide is solely intended to be information and educational in nature. Please consult a medical or health professional should the need for one be indicated. Deborah Vogel and White Owl Publishing disclaim responsibility and liability for any damages, including consequential and special damages, arising out of or in connection with your use of *Tune Up Your Turnout: A Dancer's Guide* whether based on contract or tort.

ISBN 0–9766084–0–5

Acknowledgements

There are so many people who have supported me throughout my life and its various adventures. I am particularly indebted to

- Doris and Frank, my mom and dad, for their never-ending love and support.
- Gwen, Pam & Craig, my siblings who help me even when I am "way out there".
- Irene Dowd, my amazing mentor, for teaching me how to "see" movement.
- Nusha, Carter, Judy, Carol M. and Tim, for their guidance and friendship over the past 3 decades.
- The dancers, dance teachers, clients, and students, past and present, who taught me how to listen.

Namaste

To my children, my manna from heaven,
Erika Caitlin, Ian Christopher & Dylan Mariah

Contents

Turnout Basics

Is it still possible to improve my turnout? I'm 18 years old, have fallen in love with both ballet and modern and am concerned that it is too late for me to pursue a career in dance.

Sincerely,

Dylan

It is often thought that you have to be born with the "right" body in order to pursue a career in dance. I believe that it is more important to have the right information in order to maximize your ability to use what you were given. It is possible to improve how you use your turnout no matter what your age. The way to do that is to evaluate your muscular balance around the hip joint, put it together with what you know about your structure and habits, and learn to effectively stretch and strengthen the turnout muscles. That is what this book will teach you to do.

Dancers constantly evaluate themselves and others by a physical yardstick: How much turnout do you have? How high is your extension? What is the curve of your foot while pointing?

Turnout is the ability to rotate the leg outward at the hip. Turnout is a concern of all dancers, whether they are ballet, modern, or jazz based. Dancers are unique in that they constantly try to find new ways to "look" as if they have more turnout, than what they have structurally in the hip.

The most-often asked question about turnout is: Can I improve what I've got? Or is my turnout determined by my anatomical structure, so what I was born with is what I have to work with?

The answer is you can always improve how well you work with what you have. More often than not I have seen dancers who were unable to utilize their full turnout because of inefficient muscular patterns. Typically, the inefficient pattern is one of strain, by creating artificial turnout at the knee and ankle instead of at the hip. It is not unusual to find dancers with so much tension in the turn-out muscles that they can't use their full range of motion.

In this guide you'll learn:

1. Where turnout actually occurs in the body, and how to test for it.
2. The important structural components of the hip joint.
3. To identify alignment issues that interfere with efficient and effective turnout.
4. How to increase the range of motion at the hip by balancing the flexibility and strength of those muscles that create turn-out, without compromising the body.

It takes a lot of hard work to become a proficient dancer, but it should not create pain or injuries if one works within the efficient anatomical design of the body in movement. When you watch professional dancers perform on stage or on video you begin to realize there is a large range of functional turnout that is used, meaning that even professional dancers aren't always working at 180 degrees of turnout.

Our favorite dancers are the ones who are able to commu-nicate the grace and beauty of the movement throughout their entire bodies, not just at the hip joint. Realize that the goal behind using turnout efficiently is to increase a dancer's ability to DANCE—which goes far beyond their ability to stand in a perfect plié at the barre.

When a dancer comes to me for help with her turnout I always start with the following baseline evaluations.

1. Look for variations in their standing alignment.
2. At what range of turnout/turn-in do they test?
3. What is the range of flexibility and/or the state of weakness or strength in the muscles that influence turnout?

4. What are the dancer's movement and alignment compensations that they use to create more turnout?

Looking at these four areas and working with any imbalances you find will definitely improve your ability to work more efficiently with your turnout.

Remember that the goal of barre work is to prepare the dancer for center combinations and moving across the floor, which prepares them for performance. Dancers need to work with a "realistic turnout" to prepare themselves for center and across the floor combinations.

The most important reason to understand the anatomical issues around turnout is so the dancer will have a long and healthy career; minimizing the potential for injuries at the hip, knee and ankle.

Question: Understanding Swaybacks

Why is it so hard for young dancers to stand with their pelvises upright instead of in a swayback?

Angie

We know that the pelvis is bowl shaped, and the common pattern for young children is to stand with their bellies poofed out, in a swayback position. When you are in that position, the hip flexors are in the shortened position, and the extensors of the hip are in an elongated position. If this is the posture that most children come from (think toddlers and their bellies) then what has to happen for them to begin to stand with their pelvis more accurately aligned on their legs?

It's a combination of muscular events. The more active a child is, then the more they naturally begin to use their abdominals for

Swayback

support. Climbing trees and playing on the monkey bars, walking along the fence, playing hide and go seek, were once big-time activities for growing children. Children didn't always have the amount of inside activities as they do now with the computer, the video games, TV. Being outside, riding bikes, and plain old ordinary play has important ramifications in their gaining abdominal strength. The amount of sitting children do at school and in front of the TV and computer does impact on their overall physical health.

Dance class for young bodies is a wonderful way to support good alignment, but can't take the place of running and other cardiovascular "playing".

The abdominals help to create the front of the pelvic bowl and keep it from tipping forward. The extensors of the hip will help keep the back of the pelvis from riding up. When the hamstrings and other extensors are weak the young dancer will tip her pelvis first before doing a tendu to the back, for example. To do a proper tendu to the back requires abdominal strength to counter the tendency of the pelvis to tip into a swayback, as the hamstrings and gluteal muscles draw the leg behind.

Remember that you must always look at both sides of a joint when evaluating movement. The hip flexors need to lengthen as the hip extensors bring the leg backwards. If the hip flexors are tight, you won't be able to keep the pelvis upright and the hamstrings and other extensors won't be able to work as well.

If the hamstrings are overly tight and the dancer is tucking the pelvis under with the gluteals, then they are going to have trouble stabilizing the pelvis in the upright position. For example, we know the gluteals and hamstring muscles have to contract in order to take the leg behind—it is impossible to do a tendu to the back without having them contract. But if you are tucked under, you will shift forward on the standing leg instead of being centered on your foot. This compromises your alignment.

Tucking the pelvis and/or standing in a swayback position can lead to the tendency of sinking into the standing hip when you shift onto one foot. Both patterns limit the mobility and the moveability of the dancer. Often you will see young dancers locking their knees when they are tucking their pelvis under. This also makes it challenging for them to find the deeper rotators in the hip to turn out their legs.

So what are some ways that we can help our young dancers find the correct placement of their pelvis on their legs?

One trick is to have them stand with their pelvis lightly touching a wall. Their shoulders should not touch at all—even the skinniest of dancers have some pelvic protrusion. When they are doing their demi-plié, they'll keep the gluteals lightly touching the wall as they slide down, keeping the weight even on the three points of their feet, and without the shoulders touching the wall. You might give them the image of a merry-go-round horse sliding up and down on the pole.

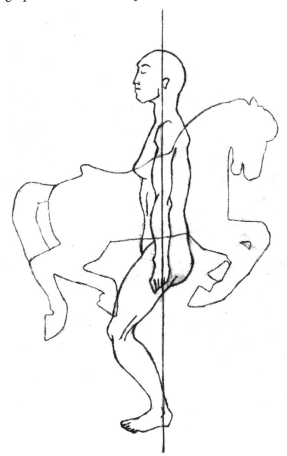

Merry-Go-Round Alignment

We need to find fun ways for young dancers to strengthen their abdominals. One way is by using the physioball in class doing simple stabilization exercises. (A great book for physioball work is *Pilates on the Ball* by Colleen Craig. I don't get anything by endorsing her book, it's just one that I like a lot.)

We need to help them find strength in their hamstrings and can do that in a variety of different ways. A very simple exercise is to have them lie on their stomach and think of their belly button lifting up towards their spine. Then have them barely lift one leg off the ground, and then the other—like a flutter kick in swimming. They don't want their lower backs to tip into a swayback, which is why they are focusing on keeping the abdominals engaged by lifting their belly button, and not lifting their legs up very high. It doesn't take much to get the high hamstring attachment going. They will feel this at the top of their leg, around the sits bone area.

Have them stand back up and imagine themselves like a flexible tube, getting long and skinny like Gumby. That should help them find the vertical line of the body, instead of lifting their ribs as a way of standing up straight.

When in doubt, stretch the hip flexors, strengthen the extensors, and this will help align their pelvis. Before they begin any dance movements they need to be in neutral, which is having the pelvis aligned efficiently over the legs. This way the weight of the body will transfer through the bones of the legs, rather than having the muscles supporting the body instead of moving it.

Question: How to Find Turnout

When working with children ages 9–11, what is the best way to get them to understand and feel how turnout originates in the hip? I have some exercises to help them feel it (holding it from demi-plié, lying down and doing Rommett-like exercises) but how do you describe the feeling with descriptive analogies? Any ideas?

Many thanks for your help.

Deidre

By isolating the rotation of the hip joint for them to experience, you're working with them in the right direction. Start them sitting on the ground with their legs straight in front of them. Begin by having them put their hands lightly on their thighs, right above their knees, or even over their kneecaps and have them do ankle circles with their feet. The focus here is to move their feet at the ankle joint without having them move the upper leg. The goal is specificity and disconnecting the habit of turning the feet out without turning out from the hip.

Then we turn our attention to the hip joint.

It's easier to start having them observe their feet and once they have mastered that you can ask them to turn the legs in and out from the hip without using the feet as a visual guide. The action is similar to a windshield wiper. I would have them initially do this with their feet in a flexed position. When they are in that flexed position you can use the image of windshield wipers, or of opening and closing a book. Think of a hardcover children's book, resting the spine of the book on the floor and opening it from the middle. Mention that most dancers will only open the book to 45 degrees or a little more, so they don't think they are going to be opening the book flat on the floor.

Have them begin by sitting up so they can watch their legs for a few times, and then lay them down on their backs and repeat the above; first doing ankle circles without the hip involvement, and then moving their legs like windshield wipers while monitoring their lower back to keep it from arching or tucking.

Notice they may have slightly more range when they are sitting up and doing the windshield wipers versus lying on their backs. That is because everyone has more range in their turnout when their hips are flexed.

Stirring soup is a good image for working the leg in passé. Let's say the students are lying on the ground on their right sides with their foot in a straight line from their hip. It's the top left leg that will be stirring the soup. Have them bring their left leg up into passé and slowly make circular motions as if the left femur was a spoon and the head of the spoon went deep into the hip socket. It makes them really use the turnout muscles. Don't worry about the foot staying in contact with the knee as long as it stays close to the thigh, but instead have them monitor whether they are staying on the side of their hip and not allowing themselves to roll on the backside of their pelvis, which would be the equivalent of turning out the left hip too far and losing the turnout in the right hip.

Their bottom leg can be bent to stabilize their position while they are working the top leg "stirring the soup," moving the leg in a circular motion. This works their turnout nicely, and also helps them feel how to stabilize their pelvis as they keep themselves from rolling backwards on their hip.

Stirring the Soup

Tips from the Field

"Some teachers have their students make a mock hip joint with their hands, one hand forms the acetabulum and the other is in a fist representing the head of the femur. They will have the fist placed inside of their lightly cupped other hand. Then they can rotate the fisted hand inside of the other to show how the femur moves in the hip joint." Another great idea is to describe the action of rotating the thighs in plié like the stripes on a candy cane to promote the understanding that rotation is an action, not a position.

Other teachers use rotator disks for helping young students find their turnout. (You can find these at www.pilates.com. Click on small items, then discs and boards.) They are used with dancers to show them how to find their turnout by turning out the whole leg while maintaining a straight leg. These discs are wonderful aids to have at the studio. It doesn't take many repetitions for a dancer to feel how they must keep their weight even on their feet as they turn out at their hips.

Another useful aid for understanding turnout is a small, model skeleton. It's fascinating to see where the joints are and how the bones move. I have found a good source for a 33½ inch tall budget skeleton at www.anatomical.com. Pictures are worth a thousand words, and *The Anatomy Coloring Book* by Wynn Kapit is a fun way to learn about muscles.

CHAPTER two

Anatomical Alignment

Let's begin by describing the ideal alignment of the dancer's body. From the front, the weight of the body runs down through the spine to the pelvis, and continues down through the bones of the leg. The bony skeleton is what should be carrying the weight of the body, not the muscles. When we look at the dancer's legs from the front, we should first see if the hip, knee, and ankle joints are in line with each other.

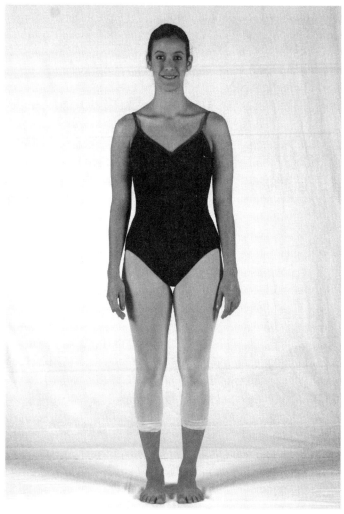

Front Standing Alignment

Looking at a dancer from the side, we look to see whether the ear is over the middle of the shoulder, which is over the middle of the hip, knee and ankle joints. This alignment is fairly simple to see when the dancer is standing in parallel; it's a little trickier, when they are standing in a turned out position.

Side Standing Alignment

Next, with the dancer in first position, look at the alignment from the front. You are looking at the facing of the knee and the line of the foot. Note any discrepancies: is the foot turned out more than the knee? If you drop a line from the knee to the ankle joint would they match up, or is the knee inside of the ankle?

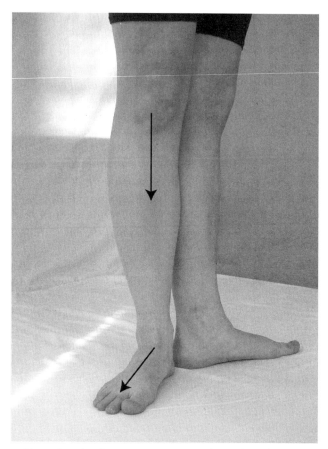

Note that the feet are more turned out than knees.

These are the baseline skeletal markers that identify the ideal alignment for dancers (as well as non dancers.) In the next chapter let's look at how the hip joint is designed, and the muscles that influence turnout. Then we will look at some of the many variations you might see in alignment and explain how they will influence your ability to utilize your turnout.

three

Anatomy of the Hip Joint

The hip joint is a ball and socket joint. The thigh bone, or femur, is the long bone of the upper leg. At the greater trochanter, which is the bump that is felt on your outer/ upper leg, the bone angles inward towards the pelvis. This area is called the neck of the femur. The femur ends as a ball-like head which fits into the concave portion of the joint called the acetabulum.

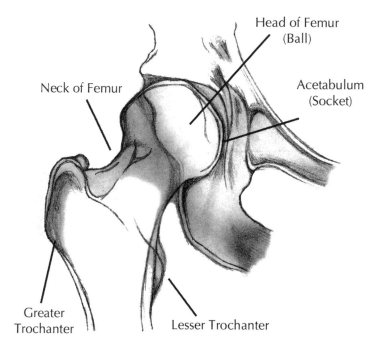

Hip Joint

This ball and socket joint has a wide range of motion. It is one of the most secure joints in the body and is very difficult to dislocate.

There is a ligament that goes from the middle of the acetabulum (or socket) to the head of the femur. This helps to anchor the femur securely into the socket.

To find where the hip joint is located on your body you would flex your thigh and feel the quadriceps tendon that pops up. Then put your finger just to the inside of the tendon. Imagine dropping in 2–3 inches and you would be where the head of the femur meets the acetabulum. Usually you can span the width between the two joints with one hand.

The great trochanter is the prominent bump that you feel on the outside of your thigh. If you run your hand across the side of your thigh as you are sitting you will feel the bulge of the greater trochanter. Now each dancer will have more or less padding around the hip which will influence how the leg looks, but for the most part, the angle of the femur is what each of us is born with, and that will not change.

The lesser trochanter is the smaller bump that is way up high on the inside of the thigh. This is where the iliopsoas muscle attaches. We will talk about the iliopsoas muscle in greater detail later.

While all hip joints are ball and socket joints, the shape of the socket, or acetabulum, into which the head of the femur fits may vary. You may have a very shallow socket, which would allow a greater range of motion and turnout, but also leaves the joint slightly more vulnerable to dislocation and other joint problems.

Of all the dancers I've tested over the past 23 years—only a few tested with "180 degrees of turnout" or "Turnout to the Extreme." Most of these dancers had shallow sockets that were confirmed by x-ray.

They had come into the clinic with other types of problems primarily related to stabilizing that great range—just to keep from dislocating the joint. We don't hear of many TRUE hip dislocations. I personally only know of two dancers that have dislocated at their hip joint; it is really hard to do.

Hip dislocation is different from a "snapping hip" that you will sometimes find with dancers. Snapping hip syndrome is named for the clunking sound that occurs at the greater trochanter when the dancer stands and shifts their weight onto the leg, which creates the snapping sensation and clunking sound. Extremely tight lateral hip muscles create this clunk as they snap over the greater trochanter. This is not a desirable action as it's an easy way to develop bursitis or tendinitis in the greater trochanter area over time due to the constant irritation. The solution is to stretch the lateral hip muscles.

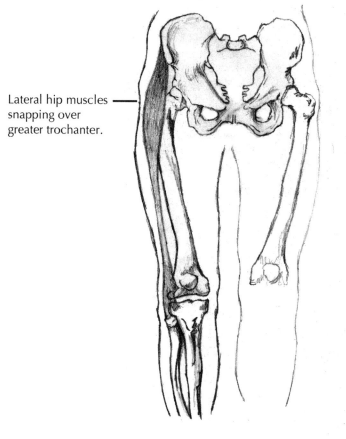

Lateral hip muscles snapping over greater trochanter.

Snapping Hip

On the other end of the turnout spectrum, you may have a very deep hip socket that would limit the range of turnout, as the head of the thighbone would more quickly come in contact with the edges of the socket.

Probably the most important structural influence to turnout is the angle of the neck of the femur to the pelvis. You can be in a normal range, or have the neck of the femur be anteverted (turned in) or retroverted (turned out). We will evaluate those structural influences in the next chapter.

Testing Turnout

Most dancers will have a normal hip structure, in which the amount of turn-in versus turnout is generally in balance. Usually, about 45 degrees for both is the norm. This is where the majority of dance students will test.

However, as we move into the arena of professional ballet companies, we'll find there is more turnout present in this portion of the dance population than turn-in. One might assume that only those with more than average turnout will become professional dancers—but that is certainly not the case. There are many beautiful professional dancers in all areas of dance who have less than ideal turnout, and it is the goal of this book to help all dancers maximize their turnout while minimizing injuries.

How to Test for Turnout

You want to test for turnout with the hips in an extended position, so begin by having the dancer lie on their stomach, with their legs stretched straight behind them. The reason to use this position rather than the frog position is that everyone tests with a greater range of turnout when they are in a flexed position. What is more important is how much turnout a dancer has standing in first position. (Another reason why not to bend your knees, plant your feet into first and then stand up. Too many young dancers "screw their knees" to create turnout and risk damaging their knees when they do that.)

As I test someone's turnout I make sure that their hip doesn't come off the ground as I bend their knee. I do that by gently keeping one hand on the back of the pelvis in order to monitor any movement. (If the hip moves away from the floor as you bend their knee it means they have tight hip flexors and will want to address that through stretching the quadriceps and iliopsoas muscles.)

Once their knee is at 90 degrees, let it fall gently over their other knee. This is gauging their turnout.

Testing Turnout

Then let the knee fall gently away in the opposite direction, this is their turn-in.

You are approximating the angle of turnout and turn-in, which for the majority of people will be 45/45 as an average amount of turnout. You have a baseline reading of the dancer's turnout now. Does it mean that you can't increase it? No, of course not. There

Testing Turn-in

are many influences to turnout and the goal is to improve your ability to utilize your turnout without injury. Periodically you may want to retest to see if any changes are occurring as a result of your efforts in strengthening and/or stretching the muscles. Having a baseline measurement is useful for this.

I mentioned earlier that the frog position is not an accurate measurement of turnout. The following pictures were taken with a dancer who tested with less than average turnout and more than average turn-in. Her turnout tested around 20 degrees, and her turn-in tested 65 degrees. See how much greater her turnout appears to be as she lies in the frog position in comparison to testing her turnout with the hip extended.

True range of motion at hip measuring 20°.

Frog position shows inaccurate range of turnout.

Question: What's up with the "Frog Position"?

Does the frog position (lying on abdomen with feet touching in a diamond shape) serve the dancer any purpose? My 10-year-old daughter has a dance teacher that has the students stay in this position for a few minutes each class. She finds it very uncomfortable.

Thanks,

Joanne

Sometimes it is hard for dancers, especially young dancers, to know how to evaluate the situation when something is uncomfortable. Is it uncomfortable because it is a new stretch, or is your body trying to tell you something is not right? Often when you are trying something new, or working in a way that your body is not accustomed to, you will feel some discomfort. Don't immediately jump to the conclusion that the position or stretch is injurious to your body.

However, this is one of those times that your daughter's discomfort is unnecessary and truly a signal that her body does not like the strain being put on it.

The frog position, lying on your stomach, or on your back, is not useful for increasing turnout. In fact it can be injurious to your knees.

When you are lying on your stomach with your legs in a line underneath, your hips are in extension. Flexion is when the angle at the joint is decreasing; for example, when you bring your knee up towards your chest it is flexing. Extension is when the angle of the joint is increasing. An example at the hip would be returning your leg from a flexed position or taking the leg behind you as in a back tendu.

Consider standing in first position: where do the majority (99% of the dance population) have their feet pointed? As close to pointing straight side as possible. In my 25 years of working with dancers, I have tested only 3 dancers who had an anatomical turn-out that totaled 180 degrees. Average turnout is 90 degrees, with each leg turning out 45 degrees; in the dance population it may be a bit more.

When you are lying on your stomach and begin to take your legs out into that diamond shape a couple of things happen. One, if you are tight in your hip flexors you are going to begin to arch your back and lift your hips slightly off the floor. This puts more pressure on the inside of your knee which is made more vulnerable by the fact that you have it bent and are trying to put your feet together and on the floor.

The knee is in an extreme torque—you are putting strain on the ligaments and cartilage—not something I want to do with any dancer, and certainly not with a dancer who is growing.

There will be dancers who have more "natural" turnout, which is called a retroverted hip structure, who will be able to lie on their stomach and begin to take the knees out to the side without dis-comfort, but then we are still asking them to torque at the knee and bring the feet down towards the floor—still not good for the knee, ever. It is the equivalent of standing in extreme pronation, with the foot overly turned out and the knee twisted outwards, because unless you have 180 degrees of turnout, you cannot ana-tomically create that position at the hip.

Doing the frog position lying on your back and opening up your thighs into the diamond shape is less injurious to the dancer's body. If you are just resting in that position you will feel some stretching happening to the inner thigh area in the adduc-tor muscles. Do NOT ever allow anyone to even gently push the knees open in this position. I have had dancers who have had either a deep adductor muscle torn, or strained the iliopsoas tendon when someone pushed their knees open.

Old habits die hard, even in the dance world, and I am not sure when or where this myth that the frog position helps your turnout got started. I do know that it is still around as confirmed by your question.

As far as your daughter and her teacher: I would inform the teacher that after talking with a dance medicine specialist it was advised that when it comes time to do the frog position that your daughter be allowed to roll over on her back and do it in the supine position (and take it for the gentle stretch that it will provide—tell your daughter to keep her lower back lengthened so her back doesn't arch when she does it). If her knees feel uncomfortable doing the frog position on her back, then—no more frog position for her. She'll just have to stretch something else during that time in class.

Kudos to your daughter for recognizing that it didn't feel right and for you for researching further.

Other Dancers' Experiences with the Frog Position

"I knew all along that the "frog" stretch was bogus! It hurt me in all kinds of places. I also get a lot of torque in my knees in the seated "butterfly" position. My knees don't go all the way to the floor, so gravity just takes my lower legs and twists them away from my knees. If I do this stretch at all, I either consciously keep my lower legs aligned, or put pillows, (or, in class, rolled up garments that I've removed at barre!!) under my knees. All in all, it's pretty useless."

Sincerely,

Susan

"Had a teacher years back who told the class he had gone to sleep lying on his stomach in a bent knee turned out position to increase his turnout. When he woke up he was in pain and couldn't move.

Had to wait for help to come so he could even turn over. An honest & very good anecdotal warning for some of the students he saw stretching in that manner for extended periods before class. The no pain, no gain philosophy dies hard—but you're doing a good job putting it to rest."

Thanks

Diane

chapter four

Structural Challenges To Your Turnout

The Anteverted Hip

The young dancer who "W" sits or walks "pigeon toed" will typically test with more turn-in than turnout at the hip joint. This indicates an anteverted hip structure. Anteversion means the head of the femur is more anterior than the neck of the femur, which creates the inward rotation of the knees and feet.

W Sitting

When you are testing a student with an anteverted hip structure they will test with a far greater amount of internal rotation than external rotation, as shown in the following pictures.

All babies are born with a small amount of inward rotation of the thigh bone, and this generally works itself out during the first few years. By the age of 8 the angle of the neck of the femur to the head is pretty well set and after that time you want to focus on keeping a good balance in the muscles that surround the hip joint.

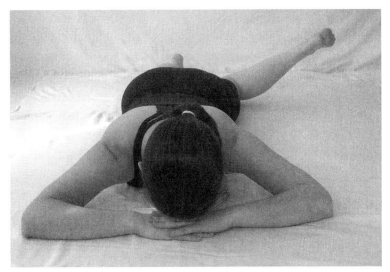

Testing Turn-in

Testing Turnout

A student with anteverted hips will have their knees looking in towards each other when their feet are parallel. This type of hip joint makes it more challenging to work in turnout in a ballet class, but as long as the student doesn't push their turnout to look like everyone else's at the barre, they should be fine.

This dancer will never have the ideal 180 degrees of turnout that many teachers want. Her problem will be discovered when she is at the barre and trying to push her feet into more turnout than what she has at her hips. This will create torsion at the knee, affectionately called screwing the knee, which over time will create problems for the ligaments and cartilage around the knee.

Dancers with anteverted hip joints don't need to hang up their dancing shoes. If they can work their first position more at a 45–degree angle, this will help to keep their ankles, knees and hips working evenly without strain at the knee and ankle joints.

If you watch videos of professional ballet dancers you will see them working with less than 180 degrees of turnout as they are going across the floor and performing. Ideal turnout does not automatically create great performers. Great performers dance with their whole body, not just their legs.

When I was in my early 20's in New York, trying to make my fame and fortune as a dancer, I took ballet class with Maggie Black. She was a well-known and very well-respected teacher. Dancers from Joffrey, ABT and SAB would come take class with her. Her barre was composed of simple movements. Combinations such as two demi pliés, grande plié, cambre forward in each position. One day I stood behind one of the soloists from the Joffrey ballet and was astonished to see the small first position he worked in. Just over 90 degrees. When he went away from the barre and started dancing the combinations in center I never noticed his first position as I watched his graceful and powerful movements. This was an important lesson for me as a young dancer—turnout at the barre does not necessarily dictate your performance or ability to be a professional dancer!

The anteverted hip may even be preferable for some sports such as martial arts and basketball. It's not that it is a "bad" or wrong type of hip joint—just more challenging to work with in dance.

The Retroverted Hip

The opposite variation to the anteverted hip is the retroverted hip joint. These are the dancers who naturally turn out their feet while walking and when they go into parallel position *feel* as if they are turned in. In fact, it may be uncomfortable for them to work in parallel, and they'll find one or both of the feet slowly beginning to turn out during pliés, for example. These young dancers "walk like a duck" with their feet turned out, even when they aren't in class.

Like anteversion, retroversion is created by the angle of the neck of the femur to the shaft. It is a structural variation you are born with. For dancers, especially ballet dancers, a retroverted hip structure means that they naturally have more turnout than turn-in.

Dancer with retroverted hip joint tests
with far greater turnout and minimal turn-in.

While some amount of retroversion will aid the dancer's quest for 180 degrees of turnout, it is not the defining requirement to becoming a successful dancer. Your structure defines the foundation for your turnout, but the dancer must learn how to work in a muscularly balanced fashion in order to fully utilize that turnout.

Whether you start with average turnout, or more turn-in or more turnout at the hips, you must still learn to use turnout correctly at the hip joint (instead of cheating and creating more turnout at the knees and ankle joints). You must also maintain good muscular balance around the hip joint in order to maximize your range of motion while minimizing your chances of injury. We will go into how to do that in the following chapters.

Hyperextended Knees

Hyperextended knees go beyond neutral at the joint. In the average dancer without hyperextended knees, when they stand with their knees fully straightened the hip, knee and ankle are in a straight line. When a dancer who has hyperextended knees straightens their leg, the knee is behind the hip and ankle, giving the legs a curved-back look.

A simple test to identify hyperextension at your knees: Try sitting on the floor with your legs straight in front of you. Lock your knees and see if your heels come off the ground. Normally, you never want to "lock" your knees, as it jams the kneecap back into the joint, but we are doing this as a test. If your heels come way off the floor you have a fair amount of hyperextension. Most of us will barely lift the heels off the ground.

Many dancers like the look of the hyperextended knee in arabesque and développés. Taking the leg into hyperextension (when it is in the air and non-weight bearing) is not a problem at all. The problems appear when the dancer pushes into hyperextension

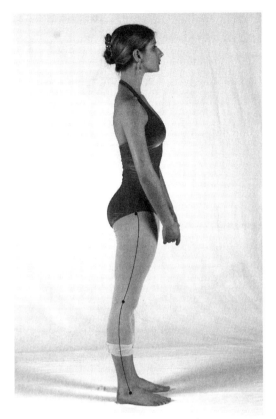

Hyperextension—Standing

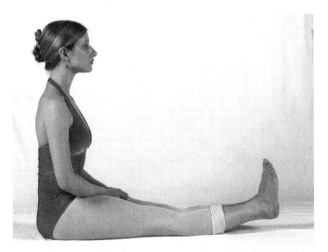

Hyperextension—Seated

while standing on that leg. They do that at great risk to the ankles and knees, making them vulnerable to injury.

A very good reason I don't promote having a dancer stand with hyperextended knees is that upper thigh (or femur) is actually turning in as the knee goes backwards into hyperextension. This is definitely working against your goal of increasing your turnout.

It's very challenging for dancers to learn to overcome the feeling that their knees don't feel straight—but they will gain strength, efficiency and a longer dance life if they can correct this pattern in standing.

Hyperextension is more   Hyperextension is corrected
pronounced on left leg.   in first position.

Know that the goal for efficient alignment is to have your turnout determined by the hip joint with the knees and ankles working at the same angle. Any major deviation from that will create problems for the knees and ankles.

Tibial Torsion

The tibia is the primary shinbone. You have another long bone in the lower leg called the fibula—it's lateral, or outside of the tibia. The term "tibial torsion" describes what happens when the tibia rotates during bone growth. It can internally rotate (turn-in) or externally rotate (turnout).

Tibial torsion could be genetic or there could be physical activities in the child's life that have caused or contributed to the rotation.

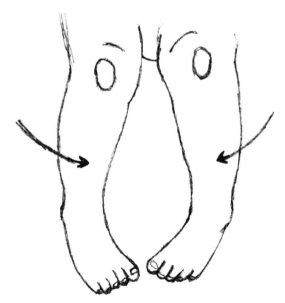

Internal Tibial Torsion

When you see a young child with an internally rotated tibia their knees will face forward while they walk with a toeing-in gait. These same children are often quite comfortable W-sitting and sleeping on their stomachs with their feet turned in, their big toes close together. While they may be comfortable W-sitting, it does create an undesirable torque on the knees, so should be avoided.

If their knees face inward and they walk toe-in, they probably have anteversion of the hip joint. They would test with more turn in than turnout at the hip. With internal tibial torsion they may have a normal range of turnout at the hip, but they will have trouble standing in turnout because the knees and ankles don't line up. Often this internal tibial torsion self corrects by age 8 through the child's normal activity.

The externally rotated tibial torsion is less common in children—with the exception of the dance community. I have found a fair amount of external tibial torsion in dancers who started ballet at a young age and did not understand how to work with the turnout at the hip, and were turning out the feet to create better turnout. It is the over-turning out of their feet that promotes the tibia to rotate outwardly in order to compensate for the stress that is being placed on the tibia.

When you look at the dancer who has an externally rotated tibia you will see that either their knees are facing forward and their feet are slightly turned out, or if they put their feet into a parallel position, then their knees face inward towards each other.

In the following pictures you will see this dancer has more tibial torsion on her right side. Notice that her knees are in parallel in both pictures while the feet are turned out.

It is not unusual to find that a dancer has more tibial torsion on one leg. A common pattern is for the side with tibial torsion to be generally the side with less turnout at the hip. We are not symmetrical human beings, so unequal turnout is not an uncommon finding. Often I find dancers with tibial torsion testing with

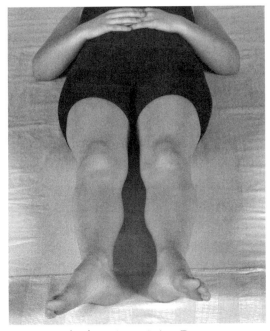

Tibial Torsion—Lying Down

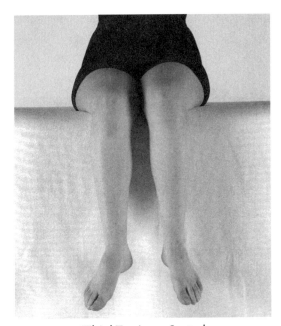

Tibial Torsion—Seated

a tighter iliopsoas on that same side. This finding makes sense, as a tighter iliopsoas would affect their ability to use their turnout, so the dancer would turn out the foot on that side to make their feet look equal in first position. (We'll talk in more detail about the muscular influences of the iliopsoas in Chapter 5.)

It is SO important for the young dancer to line up their feet with their knees and learn where turnout is supposed to happen and prevent tibial torsion from occurring. If the dancer is older and their bone structure is set, it is useful to know if there is any tibial torsion so they can learn how to work with it, instead of against it.

For example, I had a nineteen-year-old dancer in class with pretty significant tibial torsion on both legs. She was taking a modern dance class where we worked in parallel position as much as first position. She came up to me one day after class because in demi plié when her feet were in parallel her knees would hit each other. If she pulled her knees out to the side to keep them over her feet, she would have pain on the outside of the knee. She wanted to know why she was getting pain during this simple movement.

After a quick evaluation where I tested her turnout and looked at her knee and ankle alignment, we confirmed that she had external tibial torsion. She adapted her parallel position to allow the feet to turnout ever so slightly. This allowed her to access the correct turnout muscles at the hip more easily and took the strain off the knees. She was instructed to continue to think of lining up the three joints of the lower extremity and to monitor the three points of her feet. These three points were the pad of the big toe, the pad of the little toe and the heel. Her instructions were to have equal weight on all three points of the foot—which are the same directions that all dancers should follow.

When she worked in first position she easily turned out. I suggested she not go to her full turnout at the feet in order to focus on working her turnout more correctly at the hip. In time she may be able to turnout her full amount—but always she will be monitoring the weight on her feet.

The concern with young dancers and tibial torsion comes back to the importance of monitoring young dancers and how and where they are creating their turnout. This is why it is so useful to know what their range of motion is at the hip and match that up with what you are seeing in their pliés and other dance movements.

Pronation of the Feet

When a dancer is standing in first position the weight should be equal between the pads of the big toe, little toe and heel. Having the weight evenly distributed like this maintains the integrity of the arches.

Everyone has a different amount of instep. A dancer with a really high arch is said to have a great pointe, but sometimes that high arch is also a rigid arch, and more prone to ankle injuries.

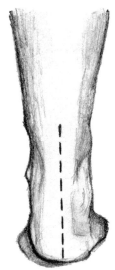

Pronanted foot   Non-pronanted foot
(Bowed Achilles tendon) (Normal Achilles tendon)

A dancer with little instep or arch is considered to have flat feet. Flat feet run in families and are more common in certain cultures, for example, the Asian and African American cultures. A dancer with flat feet can still have a strong and beautiful pointe.

Pronation, on the other hand, is a biomechanical problem. When a dancer is pronating, they are rolling in, or allowing more weight to be on the inner border of the foot, rather than evenly divided between the three points.

Pronation leads to bunions because of that increased weight on the big toe joint. Pronation can occur for many reasons, but a common cause, which follows the focus of this book, is not using turnout correctly up at the hip and instead over turning out the feet creating pronation.

The correction is to always try to stand with equal weight on the three points of the feet!

Question: Pronation

I have a few students who, when standing in first, even a relaxed first, roll in towards their big toes. I have corrected them repeatedly but they cannot stand flat. Are there any exercises that would build up the proper muscles and prevent ankle damage? Seems like their teachers in the past have stressed the "perfect first" and they are conditioned to turn out from the ankle and not from the thigh. Such a pity!

Thanks for your time. . . . Best,

Lorrie

Your students are lucky to have you as a teacher watching for the signs of pronation. This focus on making the feet appear in the perfect first turned has injured more knees and ankles than I care to think about.

Recently I worked with a dancer who had already had 2 knee surgeries by the age of 18 that I believe were the direct result of working more turned out than what his hips were able to handle. It's amazing that he is still dancing. Now that he understands what was a major reason for his knee challenges, I know his dancing is going to improve exponentially.

The first focus for those dancers is to bring their turnout in to where they feel equal weight between the pads of the big toe, little toe and heel. Then they will have a chance of working efficiently through their legs. If they continue to roll into pronation they are creating a twisting action at the knees, which are at the mercy of what happens above and below (meaning the hip and ankle joints).

There are some wonderful exercises and explanations in Irene Dowd's book, *Taking Root to Fly* in the chapter entitled "In Honor of the Foot". (For anyone who is interested I sell her book from my website.) What I would suggest as a beginning exercise is having the dancers practicing pointing without their ballet shoes on. First they are going to extend the ankle, and as they slowly point the toes they are going to try to keep the toes separated from each other and stretching long (not curling under) as they go into their pointe. The foot is a triangle shape, and as they pointe they do not want to wing the foot, which would put the big toe in line with the heel. Once the foot is non-weight bearing, they can wing if they like, but not during the tendu. Placing the foot in theraband while they practice pointing and flexing adds some resistance to strengthening those foot muscles. It can be a very useful experience to take barre in socks instead of ballet shoes every now and then, as it is easier to feel the weight on the feet, and check whether or not the toes are gripping the floor as you are standing. When you are standing in your first position or even doing a demi-plié, the role of the toes is to help balance your movement—not to lift your arch—and not to act as the glue that keeps your feet in the overly turned out position. While you are standing and working at the barre, the toes should be resting easily on the floor in their fully extended position. (Meaning that your soft slippers shouldn't be so tight that they crunch up your toes just standing in them.) The occasional use of socks instead of soft slippers will allow the dancer to feel the articulation the foot needs to go through as the tendu is executed. A tendu done correctly is a wonderful foot exercise and strengthener to the intrinsic muscles.

I encourage my dancers to roll their feet on a firm ball to release tension from the arch before they work on doming or pointing their feet. That seems to help wake up the area before they begin class. This is important whether you are a ballet or a modern dancer, or any other dance form. Our feet are generally our primary connection to the ground and we need to make sure the communication channels are open!

Getting back to the problem with the dancers who are rolling in, if they don't correct that pattern it's possible that they will end up with deformities of varying degrees to the bones of the feet. I have a vivid memory of working with a young dancer who was at SAB, whose feet on x-ray looked the feet of an arthritic 80-year-old—and she was only 15! I don't want to suggest that will happen to all dancers who pronate; certainly not, but it was a dramatic example of the worst-case scenario that can occur when dancers force their turnout. This young dancer had been pronating for years, her class schedule was intense, she had the look of a ballerina, but ultimately the punishment to her feet did her in. She had to retire from her pursuit of a dance career.

To end on a more positive note—I have seen many, many examples of dancers who began to work more efficiently with their turnout and became better dancers as a result. I like to show videos of dancers who do not maintain 180–degree turnout as they are performing. As a viewer or audience member you aren't aware of this fact because you are so immersed in their performance you don't watch them cheat and shift the feet outwards after they land from their jump or turn.

Our goal as teachers and educated dancers is to train our bodies to move in articulate ways that allow us to communicate our passion, our visions, our stories to an audience. Our bodies were designed for movement. I feel that as teachers we nurture those seeds of desire within our students by helping them to explore the depths and ranges of their unique bodies. The first step is learning how to work with what we have, and expanding those physical boundaries—not making an enemy of our physical structure, or hating it for what it isn't or doesn't have, the near anatomically impossible 180 degree turnout.

Question: How to Work with Tibial Torsion

I would like some information on the best way to manage tibial torsion, particularly for the dancer that is not working incorrectly, but has been "duck footed" from birth. I mention this because you were the first source I found that really suggested not trying to align knees and ankles for someone like this. For years teachers told me I needed to strengthen my lower leg muscles to make them align. To me it seemed that this just forced my feet to roll to the outside or put excess pressure on knees.

When you have tibial torsion you need to monitor the weight placement on your feet to determine if you are placed correctly. I understand that many teachers will say to put your knees over your feet, but the person with true tibial torsion can only do that by supinating or sickling their foot which is the opposite action of pronation, which is rolling in.

This does place tremendous pressure on the knees, and it shifts your weight backwards, making it hard to keep your pelvis placed correctly over your feet. Now we have multiple compensations occurring and an unstable dancer who is going to have trouble balancing.

As teachers, we need to constantly remind our students that the weight needs to be divided equally between the pads of the big toe, little toe and heel. Period. If you are working on lifting your instep to stay out of pronation—you lift until the three points of the foot have equal weight. Period. It's that simple.

Remember to check for tibial torsion. Have a dancer sit on a chair or table with their leg hanging down. The knee should be facing forward. Note where the foot is facing. With external tibial torsion the foot will be turned towards first position without any muscular effort (see illustrations on page 49).

In my turnout video there is a great shot of a young dancer who has tibial torsion only on her right side. She is sitting on the floor with her legs extended in front of her. Both kneecaps are facing the ceiling and the left foot is in a relaxed point, and the right foot is off on a 35–degree angle. This young dancer had an anteverted hip structure, meaning she tested with more turn in than turnout. Her right hip had more turn in than the left, and it was her right shinbone (tibia bone) that had the external tibial torsion. Is that coincidental? I think not. She had been taking ballet for 5 years, and was standing in a first position that was more than 90 degrees total. She has since then dropped out of ballet for a variety of reasons but one of them was that her knees were giving her problems. When her mom asked me my opinion I thought her changing to another style would be useful, like jazz or hip hop where there wasn't as much focus on maintaining a turned out position.

Having tibial torsion gives you a better-looking first position than what you truly have in your hips. It's more at the barre that dancers with tibial torsion can get into trouble because of the slower movements and the greater focus on the joints of the lower leg. When the dancer with tibial torsion is moving across the floor it probably feels like less of a problem because the body will automatically compensate to keep itself balanced.

As a side note, I was looking through *Dance Spirit Magazine's* audition guide and noticed that in the majority of the stunning pictures of dancers, if you analyze the turnout on the legs in an arabesque, often the standing leg was barely turned out. These gorgeous dancers in those beautiful poses are paid professional dancers. What gives?

Demystifying turnout is the reason I wrote this book. We want to encourage our dancers to work with their turnout to the best of their abilities. This requires adaptability in how they use their turnout, depending on the particulars of the movement. Let's give our dancers the tools to work their muscles correctly and within anatomical principles. Help them to understand the realities of THEIR body—so they can bring all that joy and passion to their dancing without feeling like a failure if their body isn't perfect.

chapter five

Muscular Considerations to Turnout

Lateral Rotator Muscles

The six lateral rotators are the prime turnout muscles. They lie underneath the gluteus maximus, medius and minimus and can't be easily felt. They attach at the sacrum on the back of the pelvis and insert around the greater trochanter. When those muscles contract, your leg turns out. Good muscle tone involves being equally facile at contraction and release, with the ability to come back to a neutral state in between. It is the state of neutral, or no work, that challenges dancers. There is the thought that if you want to increase your turnout then you should practice turning out all the time—not true. What you will get is overly tight turnout muscles, which ultimately decrease your ability to use your full range of turnout.

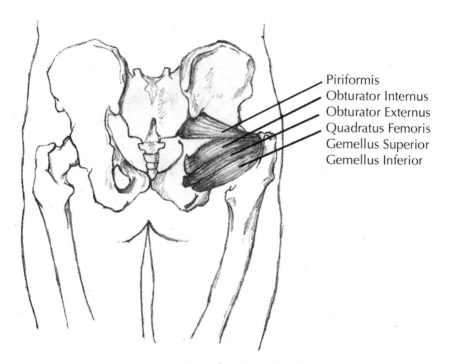

Piriformis
Obturator Internus
Obturator Externus
Quadratus Femoris
Gemellus Superior
Gemellus Inferior

Lateral Rotator Muscles

Gluteus Maximus & Lateral Hamstring Muscles

The gluteus maximus, medius and lateral hamstring are all extensors of the hip. This means that when they contract they draw the leg towards the back as in a back tendu or arabesque. If the dancer is doing any movement that brings the leg to the back, the gluteals and the lateral hamstrings will assist in maintaining their turnout in those positions.

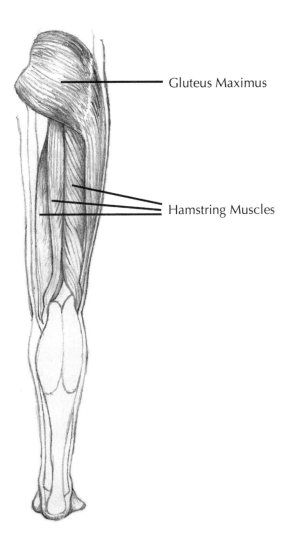

Gluteus Maximus

Hamstring Muscles

On the other hand, if the dancer is doing a movement that opposes extension of the hip, such as a plié, which flexes the hip, and they contract the gluteal muscles, then they will be tucking under. When they try to tuck under the pelvis as a way to seemingly use their turnout muscles, it feels like they are working really hard. However, what they are really doing is constantly contracting the gluteal muscles, which creates more bulk, not turnout. Not exactly the desired goal for a dancer looking for a long, lean look.

This is why the image or suggestion of pinching a dime between your buttocks doesn't help you find the correct turnout muscles. When you overuse the gluteal muscles in an attempt to increase turnout you end up compensating in your alignment by shifting the weight forward over the balls of the feet. This in turn puts more stress and strain on the knees which have to be pulled back to be over your feet. Gripping your gluteals in a plié has a negative ripple effect throughout your entire alignment. Dancers need to find the deeper primary rotator muscles underneath the gluteal muscles, working smarter, not harder.

Sartorius Muscle

Often when a dancer overuses their gluteal muscles, they will also pull into play another muscle that assists turnout: the sartorius muscle. This muscle is also known as "the tailor muscle," because tailors used to sit cross-legged on tables in order to keep their cloth from getting dirty from the floor. This muscle acts to flex, abduct and externally rotate the thigh. If we describe its actions in regular terms it would be to pull the knee to the side as your hip flexes and your thigh turns out.

Dancers, who are tucking their pelvis under, will also overuse the sartorius muscle to pull the knees back into alignment over

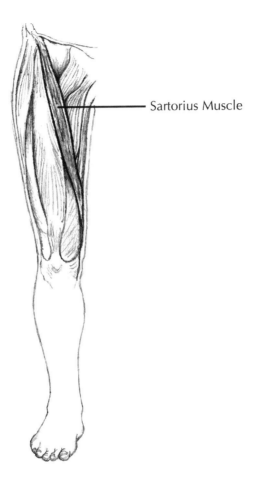

Sartorius Muscle

the feet as they are doing a plié. In some dancers, the strain on the sartorious can create a tendinitis situation where the dancer complains of knee pain. In my experience I have found sartorial tendinitis *only* in the dance population.

It is totally appropriate to call the sartorius muscle into action when you are doing a développé to the side, but inappropriate to use it to pull the knees back over your feet in a demi plié.

What are signs that you may be overusing your sartorius muscle? Most common is pain on the inside of the knee, which can be caused by problems other than overusing the sartorius.

You will see the pattern of sartorial strain watching the feet of a dancer who is pulling out their knees to the side while simultaneously lifting up the arches of their feet. This will have a tendency to push their pelvis backwards, which they counter by tucking under. That's a lot of effort just for a demi plié!

The correction to this scenario is to test your turnout, work in the appropriate first position of YOUR body, monitor the weight on your feet, and slowly work to improve your turnout without strain to the muscles and joints.

The Iliopsoas and TFL Muscle

Two muscles will influence your ability to utilize your turnout effectively when they are overly tight. These are the iliopsoas muscle and the tensor fascia lata muscle, which I will refer to as the TFL muscle.

The iliopsoas is the major postural muscle of the body. It is made up of two muscles, the psoas major and minor, and the iliacus muscle (which is the ilio part of the iliopsoas). The psoas muscle attaches along the sides of the spine from the 12th thoracic vertebra, crosses the pelvis without touching it, and attaches deep on the inside and top of the femur. The iliacus muscle attaches on the inside of each pelvic bone and joins with the psoas tendon to attach deep on the femur. The iliopsoas is a strong determining factor in both the sagittal and lateral curves of the lower spine and your standing alignment.

When the iliopsoas muscle is overly tight it will pull you into a swayback position when standing. When you are standing a tight iliopsoas muscle acts upon the spine creating a swayback, tipping the pelvis forward as if spilling its contents upon the floor.

The iliopsoas is a hip flexor and appropriately contracts along with the quadriceps as you do a tendu to the front, or any movement that involves hip flexion. When you take the leg to the back in an arabesque, for example, a tight iliopsoas will restrict the height of your leg. That sentence is worth repeating—a tight iliopsoas will restrict the height of your arabesque!

If you are standing in first position with an overly tight iliopsoas, it will act to rotate and tip the pelvis forward, which is effectively turning in at the hip joint and working against the desired goal of turnout.

If you have a dancer who knows she has a swayback, it would be a good idea to check the tightness of the iliopsoas. One simple way to see whether the dancer has a tight iliopsoas muscle is by having them lie on their back and slowly stretch out one leg along the floor—then having the other leg join the first. Watch to see if the small of the back arches significantly as the second leg straightens.

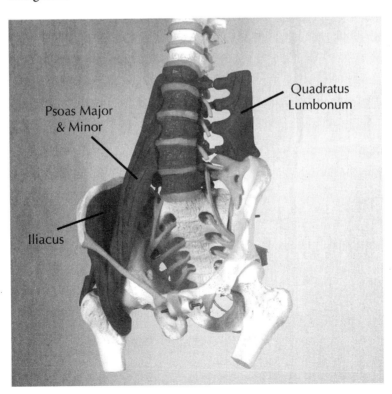

Quadratus Lumbonum

Psoas Major & Minor

Iliacus

If you're not sure whether you have a tight iliopsoas then why not test your turnout as described on page 32? Stretch out your iliopsoas muscle and test your turnout again to see if there has been any gain. A tight iliopsoas muscle is a common deterrent to turnout easily fixed by consistent stretching.

The main inward rotator of the hip is the TFL muscle. When overly contracted and tight, it will oppose the femur's ability to turn out. When you are stretching out the TFL muscle you are also stretching other lateral hip muscles. You'll feel the stretch go from the front of the hip (where you feel the stretch when stretching the iliopsoas muscle) out towards the side of the hip and the hip bone. That's how you will know that you are now in the TFL region.

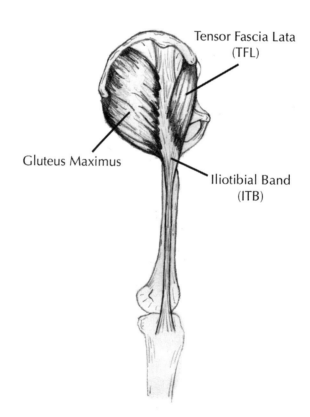

Tensor Fascia Lata (TFL)

Gluteus Maximus

Iliotibial Band (ITB)

Stretching Out the Iliopsoas and TFL Muscles

You can stretch out your iliopsoas muscle
by doing the runner's lunge.

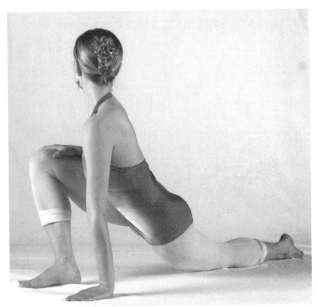

When you adapt the runner's lunge by turning towards
your bent knee, you are stretching the TFL.

This is a standing TFL stretch. The stretch will be felt on the standing leg in the outside hip.

Standing Lunge. This is an easy way to get a quick stretch of the iliopsoas during class.

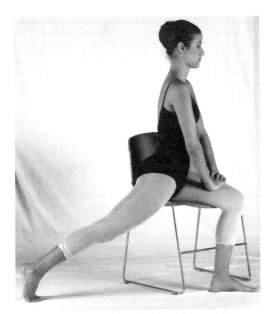

Sitting Lunge. Periodically stretch your iliopsoas
while seated at the computer or desk.

Here is my favorite way to passively stretch my iliopsoas:
allow it to hang with weight for a few minutes off a table, the top
of the stairs, or a firm bed. This gentle stretch will get stronger as
you release the weight of the leg and allow it to hang up to three
minutes.

Passive hanging stretch of the iliopsoas.

However way you stretch the iliopsoas, you want to feel the stretch in the front of the hip toward the groin. If you feel the stretch further down the front of the leg, that's fine, you are getting a stretch in the quadriceps. After stretching, most dancers say they feel looser in the front of their hips, better able to stand up straight without effort.

Like any muscle, you will have to consistently stretch out the iliopsoas and TFL muscles before you see lasting changes in their tension. We sit in flexion, walk in flexion, often sleep in hip flexion and don't spend much time in hip extension except when we are in dance class. I recommend pre-class warming up with an iliopsoas stretch to all my dancers and to stretch out when they have a moment while waiting to go across the floor during class. The iliopsoas often tightens up with repeated flexion such as battements and développés. The majority of dancers would do well to put this stretch into their daily routine even when they aren't dancing.

Question: How to Get Higher Arabesques

What are some exercises I can do to get my extensions higher, especially in arabesque?

Thanks,

Marisa

Whenever you are looking at increasing range of motion at a joint, you need to look at both its flexibility and its strength. In analyzing the arabesque typically there are issues between the flexibility of the hip flexors and the strength of the hamstrings with the hip flexors being tight, and the high hamstring attachment being slightly weak.

The first place I evaluate when analyzing a dancer's arabesque is the range of the iliopsoas muscle. At the dancers' clinic in NYC we often called the iliopsoas stretch a miracle stretch because it immediately gave 5–10 degrees more range to the arabesque after manually stretching it. Don't you love immediate gratification!

The challenge with a tight iliopsoas muscle is to find opportunities during class to take a moment to stretch, especially when movements that flex the hips are being focused on, such as battements and développés.

The easiest way to stretch the iliopsoas muscle is in the runner's lunge. You can either keep the knee on the ground or turn the toes under and straighten the knee, whichever is more comfortable. Personally, my favorite way of stretching the iliopsoas is lying on my back at the edge of a table, or at the top of a stairs. If I want to stretch the right iliopsoas, I would bend my left knee and hold toward my chest with my hands. This keeps my lower back from arching. The right leg hangs easily off of the edge of the table or stairs, and you will feel the stretch in front of the hip in the same place as you do when you do the runner's lunge. I will often hold that stretch for three long minutes to maximize the stretch.

On the other side of the joint are the hamstrings that extend the hip. In a tendu to the back you are keeping the pelvis as upright as possible while taking the leg to the back. This focuses the contraction in the upper part of the hamstrings. An arabesque is a tendu that has been raised up in back. The look of the arabesque is partly determined by the flexibility of the lower back and how upright you can maintain the upper back while lifting your leg.

A good way to work the upper hamstring is to lie on your stomach with your head resting on your hands or your face gently turned to the side. Imagine a string attached to your belly button lifting it towards the spine, engaging and lacing the abdominals including the transversus, which is the deepest layer of abdominal muscles. In this position lift your legs an inch or two off the ground and begin to do a small flutter kick as if you were swimming. The pubic bone will stay in contact with the floor with the belly button lifting away. You will feel this action high in the hamstrings, right around the ischial tuberosities, which are the sitting bones.

Now return to the standing position after having stretched the iliopsoas and strengthened the hamstrings, and practice your tendu to the back. Notice if it is easier to keep your pelvis upright while rotating and taking the leg behind. I am not a fan of over crossing the tendu to the back as it necessitates the pelvis rotating (hip opening), which then brings more of a twist into the upper back, making it harder to stay balanced on the supporting leg.

Anatomically, it is challenging enough to start in first position, and then keep the hips fairly square while going straight back into the tendu. As the leg is lifted there *must* be some rotation of the pelvis to accommodate the movement, it is otherwise impossible to lift the leg.

The better your alignment is in your tendu, the easier it will be to lift it into arabesque. The stronger the hamstrings are, the easier it will be to maintain a connection with the pelvis when doing a promenade or balancing, and not sink into the lower back.

CHAPTER Six

Increasing Flexibility

The starting point for increasing flexibility of your turnout is by first reducing tension that may be held in those muscles. An easy way to do this is through ball work. It's the equivalent of doing your own massage work. Keep the massage therapist in your budget if at all possible, but do the ball work on a regular basis in between visits. I work with a small 2¼ to 2½ inch pinkie ball, one of those dense rubbers balls you can find in the toy section of the department store or drugstore. I also have a ball collection of different sizes and firmness. If you are really sore, work with a softer, larger ball. If you want to dig deep and save yourself a trip to the massage therapist, then work with a firmer ball.

To do ball work you need a small open area by a wall and on the floor. Most often I use the wall, because it allows me to work with the ball in a variety of different settings, not only in the dance studio. Dance studio floors are generally clean and splinter-less, but there are other floors I definitely do not want to sit on! You can do ballwork on a carpeted floor as well.

You are using the ball to release muscular tension in many areas of the body. We are going to focus on the gluteal and hip area of the body. If you are interested in how to work with the ball for the upper back, legs and feet, check out my DVD *Ballwork: Releasing Muscular Tension*. This can be found at www.dancingsmart.com.

Start by placing the ball between the back of your pelvis and the wall. The farther your feet are from the wall the more weight you place on the ball and the deeper the pressure. Remember the goal is to have a comfortable amount of pressure—not pain. Begin by rolling on the ball everywhere from the sacrum (which is the base of the spine), around the sides of the pelvis, and the middle lower part of the buttocks. Remember the turnout muscles are in the middle of the pelvis, and that area may be more tender.

Ballwork against a wall or mirror.

When you hit a tender spot, you don't necessarily need to go away from that area, but simply treat it with respect. You are loosening the muscle up, getting to a state of neutral, or no work. Many dancers are so used to constantly contracting their gluteal muscles in an attempt to tuck the pelvis under and make it look smaller, that their turnout and gluteal muscles are in a constant state of contraction.

Another useful way of working with the ball for your turnout is to sit on the ball on the floor. Use your hands to decide how much weight to give onto the ball and roll from over the buttock area. Rolling all the way onto your side is a great way to release tension from the lateral hip muscles, which if you are a dancer with normal width hips, are often tight. That's a majority of dancers. Not many of us keep our prepubescent straight bodies.

Ballwork on Floor

When I'm teaching a workshop on turnout, I first teach the participants how to roughly gauge their range of turnout by lying on their stomach and rotating the thigh. Then, we'll work with the ball for about 10 minutes and go back and retest their turnout. Amazingly, at least half of the participants will test with more range of turnout after working with the ball. That's a big clue that they are actually working against themselves by overly contracting the turnout muscles. As we've talked about before, good muscle tone means the muscle is both flexible and strong.

chapter Seven

Stretching

There are many ways to stretch the turnout muscles. You can sit in a yoga stretch, a cross-legged stretch, or put your leg up on the barre in a front attitude, among others.

It is best to be warmed up before stretching. This means when you take a dance class, you want to spend some time stretching after class in order to keep the muscles lengthening as they cool down.

While it isn't harmful to gently stretch when your muscles are cool, or you're not warmed up, you will notice a greater response to your stretching when you are warm. Some of my best classes were when I had a delay getting to class on the subway and would jog (or sometimes run) to get to class on time. I'd jump into class, already slightly sweaty and very warm, and then spend time after class stretching.

While I don't encourage running into class at the last minute, I do encourage dancers to walk quickly or jog around the studio, do some leg swings, or bicycling on your back, anything to get your heart rate slightly raised and your muscles warm and joints lubricated. It takes only a few minutes, and any stretching or ball-work that you do after that will be more responsive.

When you increase the body's temperature it will improve nerve conduction, meaning that nerve messages travel faster at higher temperatures. If your reflexes and muscular reactions are faster, you will reduce the potential risk of injury. This is one reason you will find that the professional dancer spends more time warming up than the recreational dancer. A proper warm-up will improve your stretching and your performance!

In my experience, having the first pliés of the class as the warm up for your body means you are missing out on making those pliés all they can be. You want to be ready and warm for that first plié, so you can isolate and work those deeper turnout muscles efficiently. When your muscles are warm, your nervous system can pass messages more quickly, so you can respond to the small cues and sensory feedback your body is sending to you.

In all stretching, it is ideal to hold the stretch for at least one minute, and if you can take the time, up to three minutes. Often times while stretching it takes 30 seconds or more to release tension surrounding that area. For example, while doing the barre stretch you may find yourself holding tension in your neck and shoulders. As you release that tension you will feel the stretch in the hip area deepen. The goal is to isolate the desired area and focus the stretch there. Knowing where you want to feel the stretch is an important feature of teaching stretches. In stretching the turnout muscles you want to feel the stretch somewhere in the gluteal area, perhaps as low down as the sits bone (ischial tuberosity) of the pelvis. You don't want to have the majority of the stretch felt in your lower back or hamstrings, or any other place. If you do, then you need to adapt your stretching position or focus on releasing tension in the other areas first, before stretching out the turnout muscles.

Crossed Leg Stretch

My favorite way to isolate the turnout muscles is by having the dancer lie on the back with both knees bent and feet on the floor. Bring the right ankle over the left thigh and allow the right knee to open to the side. Bring the right hand between the legs and clasp both hands around the back of the left thigh. Gently lift the left foot off the ground as you bring the left thigh towards your chest. You will feel the stretch in the back of the right hip. If there is any strain in the lower back, the thighs are being pulled too close to the chest.

Cross Leg Stretch

Another variation to this stretch is to lie perpendicular to a wall and put your left foot on the wall instead of clasping it with your hands. This will allow you to take all strain out of the upper body and really focus on breathing into the pelvis and releasing any tension you might feel on the exhale.

As you are breathing and imagining softening in front of your hip joints you may feel the stretch get more specific in your buttock. That's fine—you are zeroing in on your tight spots.

Feel free to gently rock from one side of your pelvis to the other, stopping at any point. You'll feel the stretch shifting. Your best stretching position may be slightly different from the next dancer's so give yourself permission to explore your stretching.

Another variation on this same stretch is sitting on a chair with one leg crossed over the other in an open position. If it bothers your ankle bone to have it placed on your opposite thigh, feel free to cross your leg over more. This is a nice way to focus and stretch repeatedly throughout the day for a minute or so at a time. Often you will see results faster when you do this, rather than doing one long stretching session. Remember you can vary where your torso is facing to change where the stretch is placed.

You want to set up a realistic stretching routine, and for me, that means being able to stretch wherever I am, for a few minutes, without any special equipment. Consequently, I do the sitting variation most often.

Sitting Rotator Stretch

Yoga Stretch

Start by sitting on the floor with both legs straight. Begin by bending your left leg so your heel is close to your pelvis. Place the right leg over the left thigh as you rotate and twist your spine to the right. Use your left arm as a support against your right thigh stretching your spine long as you rotate.

Try to keep both sitting bones on the ground as you are breathing and holding the twist. Accommodate for any strain at the right knee by straightening that leg if necessary.

Allowing the right knee to open towards the floor and leaning your body forward over your right thigh can create a more intense variation on the yoga stretch. You don't need to lean forward very much before you will feel the stretch increase underneath the right hip area.

Yoga Stretch Variations

If your hamstrings are flexible enough, sit on the floor against the wall to help keep your spine long and erect. Your right leg will be straight while you flex your left leg towards your buttocks. Grasping your left ankle with your hand you can put your left knee inside the crook of your left elbow. Breathing easily, as you exhale, slowly bring your knee toward your chest.

Yoga Stretch Variation

You can also do a variation by lying on the floor while bringing the leg in a front attitude position up towards your chest. Remember to keep the spine lengthened on the floor and keep your pelvis in contact with the floor.

Barre Stretch

A very common way for ballet dancers to stretch their turnout muscles is by putting their leg in a front attitude up on the barre and laying their body forward over their leg. This does stretch the turnout muscles and you can again spot stretch by rotating your pelvis to face the barre more, which will increase the pull on the turnout muscles.

Barre Stretch

When doing this stretch you want to be aware of keeping both hips dropped, maintaining a square pelvic placement. It may be uncomfortable to hold this stretch for any length of time as you are putting a fair amount of pressure on the ankle that is on the barre.

Question: Flexibility versus Aging

I am a teacher who teaches 6 hours straight each day, some tap, mostly jazz. I stretch with one of my classes throughout the day. I am finding when I have my next class my hamstrings are even tighter. Any suggestions on why I feel I am losing my flexibility, which was great 2 years ago? I am a male and 36 years of age.

Thanks in advance for your help,

Rocco

Your question hit a small nerve for me, as I don't like some of the changes I see in my own flexibility. I had been chalking up the changes to not spending the same amount of time stretching now that I am teaching more than performing, so I decided to look at the research. This is what I found in *Stretching Scientifically*, by Thomas Kurz.

"Even elderly men and women over seventy years old can increase their flexibility." (Brown et al. 2000; Lazowski et al. 1999.) "With strength training the elderly, even in their 90s, can increase their strength and muscle mass—not as fast and as much as young people, but they can." (Fiatarone et al. 1990; Lexell et al. 1995.)

YES! I found other research that supported the statement that aging and decreasing flexibility or strength do not necessarily go hand in hand. But let's get real, okay? That is not the experience that most people have as they age. Why not?

The study of physiology and aging also states that as we age, our muscles and joints tend to get tighter, and connective muscle tissue shortens.

This shortening of connective tissue can influence the range of motion we have at a joint, especially if muscle balance isn't maintained. Rocco's question about his hamstrings is a perfect example of this.

Look at your lower back muscles, the iliopsoas, and the erector spinae muscles and work to loosen them up by doing the psoas lunge (runner's lunge), and the more normal rounding forward stretches we do for our spine. Often when the lower back muscles are tight, we will feel the strain in our hamstrings, and when the hamstrings are tight, that stress will be felt in our lower back. When one muscle group gets tight, the other muscle groups will try to compensate. The same pattern happens with strength. If one muscle is weaker, another muscle will try to take over some of the work—often setting up potential strain or tendinitis, etc. in the compensatory muscle.

We are very aware of muscle balance and alignment as dancers, and when we are still taking class for ourselves we continue to work on maintaining good muscular balance. Teaching, however, as our main form of exercise, does not do the same good things for our bodies, simply because we are so focused on our students as we are moving. It's been my experience that even if I am stretching with a class, I am still observing students, talking and counting as I am stretching. I'm aware of what is happening in my own body, but not truly in dialogue with it.

There are lifestyle changes that happen after the age of 30 that influence our flexibility and strength. We begin to have more responsibilities, less time to focus on our own health and well-being. Certainly, this has been a juggling act that many people—not just dancers—are faced with.

So—the good news is our bodies are adaptable and can improve flexibility and strength even after a long period away from dancing (having children, or whatever our reasons are).

The bad news is that it will take a commitment to stretching and strengthening, not twice a week, or three times a week—but small amounts daily, or as close to that as possible.

I remember seeing a report on an older woman who, when she turned 60, took up running and ran in her first marathon in her early or mid 60s. Wow! How inspiring! (Especially as I have never felt I could easily run a mile.)

My vow is not to beat up on myself for not having the body I used to have when I was in my 20s. And I take comfort in the knowledge that when I begin taking time out to stretch daily, I WILL see the results of my efforts. Jane Fonda was right on when she said if you don't use it, you'd lose it!

I'll close this response with a quote from Dr. Michael Kaplan, director of the Rehabilitation Team, a sports medicine and physical therapy clinic in Maryland, who says, "There's no reason why people in their thirties and forties and even older can't have just as much flexibility as when they were younger—or even more flexibility. A 60-year-old can have more flexibility than a 20-year-old, if she works at it and stretches."

Strengthening Your Turnout Muscles

Before jumping into the exercises for strengthening and stabilizing your turnout I'll remind you that our goal for conditioning is to prepare our bodies to do the unusual and unique movements that separate dance from pedestrian movement. Three principles need to be addressed in our strength training for dancers to maximize their efforts. The three principles are overload, specificity and reversibility. We'll start with the principle of overload.

The overload principle states that the strength of a muscle cannot be increased unless the muscles are stressed or worked beyond their normal workload. You can do this in a variety of ways. You can increase the frequency of the exercise program, the duration, or the intensity. Let's say you want to strengthen your ability to jump. You might do single leg relevés, a set of 10, 3 times a day, increasing the frequency by increasing the times you repeat it during the day. You could do one set, working your way up to more reps, allowing the fatigue of the calf muscles to determine how many you do—increasing the duration. You could also do a set of relevés, and then take that into jumping, increasing the intensity.

The principle of specificity states that the way you strengthen a muscle group should be as similar as possible to the dance movements you do in class or on stage. The example that I use most often for specificity training is abdominal exercises. Most dancers and athletes know how to do "crunches," which do strengthen the abdominal muscles, but not in the same coordination that they would be used for standing up straight, or keeping the torso tall and long while doing a développé, for example. The abdominal muscles in a crunch are doing a concentric contraction which means the length between the ends of the muscle are shortening, while the abdominals work more generally in eccentric and isometric contractions when you are standing and walking. Isometric contraction means the length of the muscle stays the same, eccentric contraction means the muscle lengthens as it contracts.

The last principle, reversibility, describes the loss of strength that happens when you stop training. This loss of strength can occur rapidly unless there is some other form of cross training to take its place. Generally speaking, a muscle needs to be conditioned at least two times a week in order to maintain its level of strength. What does this mean in practical terms? A common example would be dancers who take the summer off from dance classes. They are going to take a longer time getting back in shape come fall than someone who danced even occasionally, once or twice a week, during the summer. If they didn't dance, but worked out at the gym on a regular basis, focusing on their overall health, combining cardiovascular with weight training, they will have a far easier time coming back into classes in the fall as their general muscle tone will have been maintained but without the specificity of dance movement. Do encourage dancers to cross train for optimal health.

Two factors that influence the strength of a muscle. The first is the size of the muscle and the second is the nervous system's ability to control the muscle. Each muscle has many muscle fibers—often hundreds of thousands. When these fibers receive a message or signal from the nervous system they contract, or shorten. If the movement requires little strength, then fewer fibers will be directed to contract. As more strength is required, then more muscle fibers are called into action. Through strength training, the nervous system is learning to better coordinate the contraction of muscle fibers—this increases their strength without increasing their size. It will do this naturally when the body is in good anatomical alignment AND the dancer is not overworking their musculature. What do I mean by that? I often see dancers standing in first position, with their gluteals contracted and tucked under, their quadriceps contracted to "pull up" their knees, their arches "lifted", shoulders "pulled back", necks "lifted". Get the picture? They have incredible muscle contraction going on and they aren't even moving! Now when they move from that posture, they'll have to work even harder (with the potential to create muscle strain), or release the held position in order to move. Very inefficient muscle usage, although it does make you "feel" that you are working very hard.

A well-toned muscle is one that is strong and flexible. An example of this are the hip flexors that need to be strong to lift the leg up into a battement front, but also need to be flexible in order to lengthen into an arabesque.

There are times that cross training is a very good way to help muscles develop the strength they need for specific dance movements. For example, if you are trying to develop more strength for higher développés, doing knee extensions or leg lifts would give the quads a better foundation of strength. You can increase the number of repetitions done in one set, or increase the number of sets done throughout the day. If you put a weight around your ankle while doing knee extensions, it would increase the intensity of the exercise. Then you can get back to specificity and practice your développés while lying on your back, to keep your pelvis and torso aligned, before returning to try them in the standing position.

Sometimes dance classes cannot give you everything that you need to develop as a dancer and that is when the educated dancer does training, whether it be for strength, flexibility or coordination, outside of class.

With the following exercises we will find the turnout muscles and then focus on stabilizing your turnout on the standing leg and then with the gesture leg. By doing so, you will gain strength and control over your turnout. You will not strengthen the turnout muscles simply by walking in a turned out position (like a duck), or by constantly contracting the lateral rotators. You will most likely develop tightness and tension in those muscles rather than strength.

Finding the Turnout Muscles

Begin by lying on your side with both feet together in a straight line with the knees displaced forward. Your ankles will be in line with your hips. If you are lying on your right side, you can put your left hand on the outside of the left pelvis to monitor for glu-teal tightening.

Keeping your feet together, slowly bring the left knee up towards the ceiling. This shows you the amount of functional turnout you have—and is also a very nice way to isolate the turn-out muscles. You are monitoring your gluteal muscles with your left hand (they should be soft); you will feel the work beneath those top gluteal muscles.

Make sure you aren't opening your knee so much that you roll back on your right hip. This is the equivalent of rolling in on your standing leg, which is a common mistake that many beginning dancers make.

Slowly opening and closing that top knee while keeping your feet touching will soon activate the turnout muscles in a very clear fashion. If you are feeling fatigue after 10 repetitions it is a sign those muscles are weak. There are many variations you can do with this exercise, creating a floor-barre combination for your-self. After doing 5–10 repetitions of just opening your knee up, you could straighten the leg after opening the knee up, then work turning the straight leg in and out.

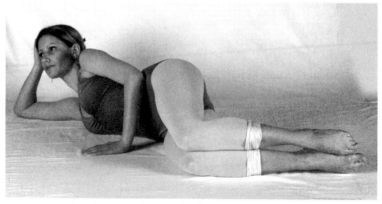

Starting position for finding turnout muscles.

Maintain hip placement during external rotation.

The weight of the leg is often enough resistance for the beginning dancer. If you want to increase the resistance for the top leg you can loop a theraband around both knees. Now as you open your knee you'll have the resistance from the theraband.

Another variation would be to start with the bottom leg bent as in the first variation, and the top leg in a straight line from the hip. If you are starting lying on your right side, then your left leg would be straight. Practice turning that leg in and out for 5–10 repetitions, keeping it in line with your hip.

Now keeping the top left leg turned out, move about 5 inches forward as if you are doing a tendu to the front, and then 5 inches behind the standing leg as if you were doing a tendu to the back. Don't let yourself roll on your right hip at all—no matter what! It doesn't take very many repetitions to feel the turnout muscles working in that left gesture leg.

When you are doing this strengthening exercise on the floor you aren't allowing any movement of the standing leg, because you are keeping the range of the gesture leg small. If you were standing and doing a tendu with your left leg, there would be some rotation of the right hip when doing the tendu to the back, but when doing the tendu to the front you should keep the hips square.

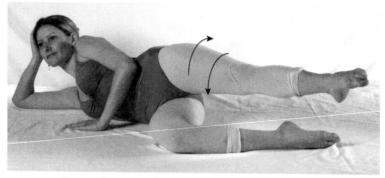

Rotate leg in and out, changing position of the
working leg without rolling onto the back of the hip.

Standing Stabilizers

The following exercises are especially good at training the standing leg to support and stabilize your turnout. Focusing on the
turnout of the standing leg will help keep the dancer from injuring knees and ankles by over turning out the gesture leg, causing
the standing leg to rotate in to accommodate the motion.

Practicing these exercises is essential for the dancers who have
a tendency to screw the knee and roll in (or pronate) at the ankle.
Over time all of these actions will create more acute and chronic
physical problems.

Gesture Leg Exercise

Begin by standing in parallel on your left foot, bending your right
leg so the foot is resting at the inside of your left ankle and your
knee is facing forward. Slowly and carefully open the right thigh
to a turned out position, as far as you can go without allowing
the pelvis to rotate. If you had an eye on your belly button you
want it facing straight forward, and not allow it to look off to the
right side. The most common pattern I see with standing turnout

is dancers allowing their standing leg to turn in as they focus all the attention on the gesture leg.

It's important to do this simple exercise with a parallel standing leg as well as in turnout. In both positions you are thinking of your pelvis as a bowl, keeping it level and lifted. You don't want to sink into the standing leg.

A good way to monitor your standing position is by monitoring the pads of your big toe, little toe and heel. Those three points should have equal weight on them. Notice if you turn out your gesture leg too far and the pelvis starts to rotate, then the foot of the standing leg will start to roll in, to pronate.

Gesture Leg Exercise
Maintain even weight on the three points of the feet.

No matter whether you are on one foot or two feet, monitoring your feet for your alignment is a good habit. Your feet won't lie. They will also tell you where your weight is. If you turn your feet out too far in first position, the inner borders of your feet will have more weight on them than the outer borders. If you turn out too far with your feet, but then "lift your arches" to make them look right you will feel the strain at either your knees or hips.

Standing Leg Exercise

The next variation to the standing exercise is to start in first position and then bring your right foot into a low coupé, with your foot at your ankle. You are standing on your left leg, in a turned out position. Keep your right leg in its coupé position and slowly rotate your pelvis on your standing leg, slightly turning in and then out. In other words, you keep your right leg in its turned out position while your pelvis turns to the left, then to the right. This is much harder than it sounds.

If you turn out the pelvis too far, you will feel the left foot starting to pronate, and strain on the left knee. Doing this exercise in a slow and deliberate fashion gives your body important practice in maintaining and stabilizing your turnout. Truly, if you keep the standing leg stabilized, then you will free up the gesture leg. You want to stabilize your standing leg with the least amount of effort. It will be harder to balance if you grip your gluteals, your hamstrings, and your toes. We want to be efficient movers. You don't need a bulldozer to move a pea, and you certainly don't want to have everything tightly engaged in order to stand on one leg.

Both variations of the standing exercise can be done on a slightly bent standing leg. Not a full demi plié, but just barely bending the knee of the leg you're standing on. This helps to

Standing Leg Exercise

isolate the turnout muscles even more, as you are less apt to grip your gluteals when the knees are slightly bent, or if you do, you will feel when you are tucking under much more quickly.

Our goal is efficiency—strong and flexible turnout—using just enough effort with each movement. Our goal is to dance smarter—not dance harder. This will keep you dancing injury free for a much longer period of time.

Question: Warm-up Concerns

I've heard some debate on how we should be warming up our dancers/athletes. Get the blood going first, then stretch? Is that the way to approach it? Also, how would you respond to a student who comes from school directly and says they're already warm because they had gym or recess? I know their body cools down in between ... who knows what time they've even had these classes? I'm just wondering what words you would use to describe the mentality behind why it is important to warm-up for dance class and not rely on those school functions. Let's say the student is younger than 12. I've had a few bicker and not really get it ... can you help?

Shereen

Good question! Students, young and old, first need to understand that warming up means exactly that. The goal is to increase the core temperature of your body and your muscles. Warming up the body loosens up the muscles, lubricates the joints and increases your energy. (Maybe you can use the example of the Tin Man in the *Wizard of Oz*.) Another example of dancing without warming up might be climbing out of bed in the morning and immediately dancing full out—their bodies would feel pretty stiff first thing in the morning until they have had time to walk around, wake up and warm up their muscles.

For the older students, you might want to add that increasing the body's temperature improves nerve conduction, meaning that nerve messages travel faster at higher temperatures. If your reflexes and muscular reactions are faster, you will reduce the potential risk of injuries. This is one reason why you will find professional athletes spend more time warming up over recreational athletes or dancers: they know it will help prevent injuries and help them compete better. The bottom line is that a proper warm-up will improve your performance.

So what is a proper warm-up?

The first 5–10 minutes should be spent in general warming up with continuous, light movement using the large muscle groups. Marching or jogging in place, doing sagittal swings, and walking briskly around the studio are all examples of the first phase of warming up. This is the phase of increasing the core body temperature.

The next phase is activity specific, and incorporates gentle stretching and targeting key areas for the activity. For example, a student taking a ballet class may want to focus on the turnout muscles and making sure they are ready for that first plié, whereas as a tap dancer would want to pay extra attention to the ankles and calves before class. Often dancers have one or two things they feel they have to do before class, and those activities would fall into this phase. For example, I need to stretch my iliopsoas before every class in order to feel that I get all that I can out of the first part of the class.

It is important to begin dance class within 15 minutes of finishing warming up, as the body will start to cool down and lose the benefits mentioned earlier. You are right in thinking that doing a gym class earlier in the afternoon, then sitting in classes before coming to dance class, will not count as their warm-up. If they have had a gym class or after-school sports activity before coming to dance class it may shorten the time spent stretching or targeting those few key areas before class, but should not shorten the generalized warm-up phase, unless they are literally within 15 minutes of coming from the other physical activity. Remind your dancers that when they watch the Olympics and they see runners or gymnasts getting ready to compete, they are moving constantly, keeping their muscles warm prior to competing, and they keep walking and moving and stretching out for a while afterwards. The cool-down phase is important for injury prevention as well as maintaining the flexibility gained during class.

I encourage you to take your younger dancers through a brief warm-up and stretching period before you begin class. Before beginning walking or skipping, ask them to describe what their body feels like. Take them through a brief warm-up and stretching, and have them describe any changes they feel. As teachers we need to help them to notice the small changes in their bodies, not just pain or lack of pain. Once they can feel positive responses to their preparations, hopefully it will encourage them to continue warming up on their own.

chapter eight

Questions and Answers

Question: How Can You Correct Swaybacks?

My daughter is 11½ years old and takes ballet many hours a week. She has always had relatively poor posture and now has "inconsistent" posture (good at times and bad at times.) She has a tendency to hyperextend her low back and has rounded shoulders and upper back. My idea is to make good posture her "norm" without nagging her all of the time. Are there certain exercises that you suggest? She may be evaluated for pre-pointe classes soon.

Thank You,

Vicki

Another Swayback Question

I enjoy reading all your articles, and the latest made me take notice. You were talking about swayback in younger dancers. My daughter is 8 and still stands that way. She is very active and takes classes in ballet a couple of days a week. Is this something that will improve with time, or is it something else . . . ?

Thanks for your help,

Treasa

We know that fast-changing adolescent bodies bring a whole set of unique problems such as self image, uncomfortable physical changes, and hormonal shifts. We know that bones grow faster than muscles and when a dancer is in a growth spurt they will need to focus on stretching their hip flexors. Our students are sitting 5–6 hours a day in class, typically slumped at their desk at school, which also promotes tight hip flexors.

So how do we get our kids to stand up straight? If nagging doesn't work, what will?

I started by speaking with my youngest daughter (age 14) who has always had good posture even though she hasn't been involved a lot with dance. (Any other dance teachers have children that don't want to be involved in their parent's favorite activity?) I asked her why she had good posture and her response was "it hurts if I don't". We went on to brainstorm what activities she was involved in ages 8, 9, and 10 and she told me that the girls' favorite activity during recess was to play "gymnastics". (We are a very small school district, there isn't any gymnastics during PE due to liability, and we don't have any gymnastic clubs or tumbling in town.) So these girls were trying, successfully, and some not so successfully, to invert themselves on their hands to do cartwheels and handstands.

I know from working with gymnasts that it takes both core control and upper back strength to do something as simple as a handstand against the wall. When you have a young child and you watch them first try to do even a baby cartwheel you can observe their wobble.

Perhaps one suggestion for our teens with bad posture might be to encourage them to do fun things like cartwheels. A mini trampoline, and jumping or jogging on that would also require them to use more core strength. Ask a child to see how high they can jump and all of a sudden you see them stretching tall as they take off.

Use the physioball as a tool for balancing out strength and Colleen Clark's *Pilates on the Ball*, or one of the many other videos and books on the subject. (Get two balls—so the teacher or parent gets in shape as well!)

You can encourage them to stretch out their hip flexors with the standard runner's lunge on the floor, the lunge stretch sitting on a chair (across the edge of the chair), the standing lunge stretch with either one foot resting on a chair or table and leaning forward to stretch the front of the standing leg, or simply in a standing lunge, thinking of lifting up the front of the pelvis as she presses gently into the extended back leg.

The focus is on stretching, not once or twice during class, but 10 times or more during the course of the day. Until the hip flexors are more flexible, the abdominal work that dancers will want to do to maintain the upright pelvis will be challenging. Releasing tight hip flexors must happen before developing abdominal strength. Then they will see a difference in their alignment over a few weeks of stretching the hip flexors, and that will encourage them to continue a steady stretching routine while their bodies settle down into their new shapes or sizes.

Besides giving the dancer many options for stretching the hip flexors I would also encourage them to sit more efficiently in their chairs. If you tell a child to sit up straight in their chair, it goes in one ear and out the other. You need to tell them to get their pelvises touching the back of the chair, which will bring them into a straighter position. Of course, that is easier to do in straight back chairs, or secretarial chairs, rather than those sloped-bottom chairs that are still around in schools, but even with those, placing your pelvis as far to the back of the chair as possible is best. Observe sitting alignments—notice that when the middle back area is touching the back of the chair, slumping of the upper body and rounding of the lower part of the body are sure to follow.

As I thought more about my own children (2 girls and a boy), I acknowledge that they have grown up with bodywork and have never hesitated to ask me for a "rub". Even in adults I have seen their body awareness shift dramatically as they became more aware that they were carrying tension and tightness. Ballwork for younger dancers would be helpful. What we don't want is for them to become so used to feeling tight or tense that it feels normal. I see plenty of clients, dancers and nondancers, who after they start doing regular ballwork, find their posture changing all on its own. (You can check out my ballwork video at my website.)

Another area of influence is backpacks. Lugging home a heavy backpack over one shoulder is not going to help their posture, especially when the pack rests halfway down their back. Heavy backpacks slung over one shoulder can influence growing spines and it is the adolescent years where scoliosis typically is noticed. Even the older, non-scoliotic dancers needs to be aware of how they carry their dance bags, as any inefficient pattern over time will create muscular tension and strain.

Question: How to Work with Hyperextended Knees

I have a ballet student with very hyperextended knees. For over a year I have been having her slightly flex her knees when she is standing and pulling up her thighs as well as keeping her weight more forward. All is going well and she has stopped having knee pain. But now she always looks like her knees are bent. How do I get her to have that lovely "super straight" look without going back into that painful locked knee position?

Lizzy

First I want to applaud you for the changes that you have made with your student. It is really hard to build the strength and muscle coordination to change the pattern of hyperextension. That is wonderful that she has learned how to "unlock" her knees for a couple of different reasons.

Reason number one is that when dancers go into hyperextension the femur (or thigh bone) is rotating inward—which goes against what they are trying to do, which is turn out the thigh.

The second reason to not allow hyperextension in the standing position is because when dancers move into hyperextension, weight drops into the heel, and often the foot then rolls into pronation, especially when they are standing in first position.

A third reason may be what your dancer was experiencing. When you have severe hyperextension you are going beyond neutral, which puts the weight of the body through the front of the knee joint. Often they will get some patellar pain, or pain that feels like it is deeper in the joint from putting stress and strain into the cartilage that is so important to the integrity of the knee.

When a leg is non-weight bearing, for example, in an arabesque, it can hyperextend as much as possible without pain. It's when legs are weight bearing that problems may arise.

I would have your student check where her weight is on her feet. Is it evenly divided between the three points of her feet (pad of the big toe, little toe and heel) or has she over compensated with more weight in the front of the foot? There may be a small amount of straightening that she can add into her standing alignment without "locking" backwards. Sometimes I will have a dancer go between locked position and then barely unlocking the knees and have them monitor their feet and their pelvis—just so they can feel how the whole body has to compensate for the hyperextension.

If her weight has shifted forward with more weight on the balls of her feet, she could be compensating with the placement of her pelvis by having to counter the forward stance with a slightly backwardly placed pelvis that may alter the look of her legs. It is not unusual for dancers to overcorrect a problem. I see it all the time—which is why as teachers we must be so careful about how we describe their ideal alignment to them. If we tell them they are standing too far back—trust me—they will often move too far forward in their attempt to correct. Instead of giving them a directional change, tell them where center or the ideal alignment will be. In this case, look for the three points of the feet with the hip/knee/ankle being in a line.

As she builds the strength in the quads to have that length and lift she wants in the legs she shouldn't push back into her hyperextension as easily as she did before. When in doubt, always monitor the feet. They will always tell the truth about a dancer's alignment.

The last suggestion I have is to watch her alignment as she is standing around talking to other dancers. Does she allow one leg to drop back into the hyperextended position? If so, encourage her to also make the changes in her knee pattern outside of the dance studio.

Question: Where Is À La Seconde?

I have a question regarding turnout in tendu à la seconde à terre. I realize turnout is turnout, however, we all have different philosophies and methods for teaching. In regards to tendu second, some teach that it is across from one's toes on their supporting side, whereas others teach it as being directly across from the supporting leg heel, which truly is side. When the body executing the tendu is aligned and lifted, then I feel this truly is the best method as it is where tendu à la seconde should be and I think it's not as easy to fake. But I prefer to teach it across from the toes of the supporting leg, as I feel this is safer for the supporting leg. I feel students are less likely to wrench their leg as they often do not use the correct musculature to maintain their turnout. Is there any validity in this manner of thinking? Is one of these less harmful than the other? Obviously I want my students to turn out, but I am always wary of injuring them and/or developing the wrong muscles that they may at some point have to undo.

Thanks,

Leigh

Great question, Leigh! I applaud you for being so aware of the nuances of tendu à la seconde. Working the gesture leg from its established first position is the best way to keep the standing leg from turning in. Turnout is always established by the standing leg.

The wrenching you are referring to happens when the student who has less than ideal turnout tries to take the tendu leg truly side and ends up either turning the tendu leg in slightly, or the standing leg even more so. We tend to notice what's happening on the standing leg less. It is natural to be focused on the movement of the gesture leg, so the more common pattern is to cheat on the standing leg for the beautifully aligned gesture leg.

Aligning your gesture leg more to the toe of the standing leg is a good goal. Often, the beginning dancer will do well to make sure they maintain the turnout they are standing in by taking the tendu in a straight line wherever their first is. This will be much more of a diagonal line, than what we think of as side.

The reason you start your beginning dancers sliding straight out from their first is to establish the pattern of using their turnout from the hip, and not changing directions as they move through the tendu. As they gain the flexibility and the stability to open their first position the angle of their tendu will reflect this.

Too often I have seen dancers begin by forcing their first position and either pronate the feet or torque the knees to stay in this forced first. Standing like this certainly compromises both the ankles and feet as well as the knees over the long term. Much better to work in a smaller first initially, and then work your way to a more open position.

Remember, if you have any question about the amount of turnout the dancer has, check their turnout by having them lie on their stomach. Then bend one knee and let the foot fall over the other leg. That is an estimate of their turnout. When you let the foot fall out away from the other leg, that estimates the amount of turn in they have at their hips. Don't allow either hip to come off the floor as you are testing.

Sometimes dancers are so good at faking turnout that you don't know there is a problem until they come to you with chronic aches or pain.

Question: What Is Piriformis Syndrome?

For at least a year, I have been having a lot of pain in my extreme lower back at the back of my hip. I have tried to release the pain by extra stretching and rolling on my ball. Recently, I was told that it might be piriformis syndrome. I have been researching it on the web, and my symptoms sound very familiar. The only thing I haven't found is a proper treatment method. I have been told two theories, (1) keep stretching and (2) try not to do anything for a few days and just ice. I was wondering what you suggest and any ideas you have for keeping it under control when I am dancing.

Thank you!

Janey

Let's start out by explaining what Piriformis Syndrome is. It's a condition in which the piriformis muscle (which is the largest of the 6 deep lateral rotators) irritates the sciatic nerve. Some people feel pain only in the buttock; sometimes it goes down the leg into sciatica, which is referred pain from the sciatic nerve.

The sciatic nerve typically passes underneath the piriformis muscle, but in about 15% of the population the nerve goes through the piriformis, increasing its potential for trouble. When dancers overwork the piriformis and the other deep rotators as they are trying to achieve more turnout, they can create excessive tension in the piriformis, which then presses on the sciatic nerve, creating pain.

Typically you are initially advised to do exactly what you are doing, resting it while icing or using anti-inflammatory medication, and stretching the piriformis muscle gently. Often times this is enough to begin to make a change, at least in the non-dance community. With dancers you should look at the bigger picture of how you are creating your turnout. Later, if your efforts are unresponsive you may need to explore more medical options.

For example, do you pronate? Pronating means you are not centered on your feet. The typical pattern I see with pronation is slightly tight hip flexors and over-developed turnout muscles and gluteal muscles. You need to examine the balance of muscle usage around the joint. Check when you are standing in first position—are your gluteal muscles soft or are you working too hard creating turnout?

You do want to stretch the turnout muscles gently, but also focus on stretching out the hip flexors by doing the iliopsoas stretch (runner's lunge) and quadriceps stretching (standing on one leg with the other bent behind you). Next you want to stretch out the tensor fascia lata, or TFL muscle, as body workers affectionately call it. You can do that by altering the runner's lunge by turning your body toward the one knee, letting the other hip drop toward the floor. You'll feel the stretch change from the front of the hip to the outside of the hip. The TFL muscle attaches on the front of the pelvis and connects into the iliotibial band.

You would also want to do the pinkie ball work on the floor or against the wall, and make sure you are going all the way to the side of the pelvis. You can also place two balls side by side on the ground and roll on them up the quadriceps muscles, and right up the side to the TFL muscle. You want to roll the ball right around the front and side of your hipbone.

You can also, when you are in class, take every opportunity to turn in. When you are watching the teacher demonstrate the next combination stand with your feet turned in toward one another, bend your knees and lean into one hip and then the other. It may look strange, but it feels good after standing in first position and helps to release the chronic tension build up in the turnout muscles.

The focus is on creating balance and getting the piriformis muscle to work in proper relationship with the rest of the muscles of the hip joint, which means being in efficient alignment. Whenever one goes out of efficient alignment, the muscles begin to have patterns of imbalance.

Question: How Can You Have Great Extensions with Poor Turnout?

A few teens were extremely flexible when it came extensions in second, side splits and side leaps. All the major muscle groups in the upper legs were stretched. However, they were very frustrated with the lack of rotation when executing a demi and grand plié. When I performed the typical rotation tests with them, I found them to have a very shallow rotation. Would you explain how this is possible and what I should look for?

Thanks,

Margie

I've seen students who appeared to have incredibly flexible side extensions, but they wouldn't have great front extensions, and then tested with average turnout when their feet are on the ground.

Let's start with looking at the side extension. Everybody (yep, everybody!) must lift the hip of the gesture leg when they are doing the side extension, otherwise, they would be limited to raising it to just above horizontal.

What happens in a side extension is that you try to keep the hips square up through passé, (let's say the right leg is your gesture leg in this example) then as you lift the knee up to set the level of the leg higher, you are lifting that same hip. When you lift that hip, it means that your weight is being shifted on the standing leg as well. You don't notice the standing leg as much as long as the dancer is able to keep the upper body upright. You do notice this natural compensation more when the dancer doesn't stay upright so that the upper body is leaning to the left.

So, the dancer who is able to keep the "look" of standing up straight appears to have the highest extension. And yes, they also have to have somewhat flexible hamstrings, although I have seen dancers who didn't test well in their hamstring flexibility who still looked like they had a high side extension.

You can't cheat the front and back extensions in the same way.

Now onto the side splits, and side leaps.

The compensation for those movements tends to be in the shift of the pelvis. Meaning, the way to compensate is to have the hip in a slight flexion. Why? Because everyone has more turnout when the hips are flexed. This is why the "frog position" is worthless when it comes to testing turnout. Everybody has more turnout in the frog position than if they are tested with the hips in extension, as in a standing first position.

Watch anybody doing a side split leap, and you will see that their legs are slightly in front of their pelvis—it's what has to happen—and it looks great when they have the strength, timing, and the erect upper body to go along with it. When we see them lift their legs at the same time maintaining an erect upper torso it looks wonderful!

Coming back to earth, standing on two legs doing a demi or grande plié, our students know they can't allow their pelvis to tip forward (which flexes the hip joint). Sometimes, they even over-compensate by tucking their pelvis under. There isn't as much wiggle room for adjustments in the standing position.

I think it is totally possible for a student to work at 90 degrees of turnout in first position (45 degrees each leg, the average amount of turnout) and still give you the beautiful side extensions because of the compensations.

Now this isn't to say they can't improve their turnout in these standing positions, they can. They release the tension, stretch the muscles, and strengthen them. It's a three-tiered approach. If you ignore any one aspect your turnout will suffer. Too much tension in a muscle, it will lose its tone. Too much flexibility without the muscular strength to support it is not good. Too much strength and tension without the flexibility is also not good.

You need all three, a strong, flexible and well-toned muscle, meaning when you aren't using your turnout muscles they release and relax. This is a good reason to do exercises that work with a range of motion at the hip by working the turnout and turn in.

Question: Increasing Hamstring Flexibility

My name is Berdien, I'm from South Africa and am 26 years old. I recently (well, a year ago) started ballet. I know this is a bit old to start, but I have always wanted to do ballet and finally got the opportunity to dance.

Now I would like to know, if you can help me with stretch exercises for the hamstrings.

Regards,

Berdien

Berdien, I'd like to congratulate you for finding the time and energy and opportunity to study dance. I so appreciate studios and teachers that offer classes for the older dancer. At a local studio in town there is a 70-year-old woman who takes ballet barre with the teen class (there is not an adult class at the studio) and still moves beautifully and gracefully. I'm hoping the teenagers in her class will remember her presence when they are older.

Hamstrings can be challenging to stretch. Try working with a pinkie ball or some other firm rubber ball against the wall or on the floor underneath the hamstring. The goal is to have the hamstrings release some of their tension before you begin to stretch them out. You might also work carefully and slowly with the ball all the way from the bottom of your foot, around the calf muscles (primarily in the back), and at the sits bone where the hamstring muscle attaches. (Properly called the ischial tuberosity of the pelvis.) The reason to massage the whole length of the leg is there is a fascial connection that runs all the way up the back of the leg, and if one area is tight, it will influence the others.

Stretch out the iliopsoas muscle by doing the runner's lunge or one of the standing variations. When the lower back is tight it can pull on the hamstrings and vice versa.

After releasing as much tension from the area as possible, you can focus on stretching the hamstrings. I suggest doing one leg at a time, and in the standing position. Put your straight leg up on a chair or the steps, slowly and gently lean forward keeping your hips square as you do so. Keeping square is especially important for women with wider hips; otherwise it is easy to miss stretching the tighter lateral hamstring by allowing our hips to slide forward instead of keeping square. Do allow the leg to turnout slightly as you're stretching which focuses the stretch towards the tighter outer hamstring muscle.

I don't suggest stretching on the floor if you have tight hamstrings as you set up an impossible situation. If you cannot sit up with your legs straight in front of you, or in second position with your spine at a 90–degree angle from your legs, then sitting on the floor trying to stretch out is only going to be frustrating and non-productive. You could lie on your back and put your legs up against the wall and rest in that position or in second position (for the inner thigh muscles) and get a nice isolated stretch without strain in the lower back.

Another way you can stretch your hamstrings is in the standing position, rolling your spine forward. If this bothers your low back muscles at all, try standing in front of a table or chair, any surface where you can rest your hands or elbows. When you do that, imagine deepening and softening in front of the hip joint. You can also bend one knee and focus the stretch onto the straight leg, and then change.

With all stretching remember that it takes time and attention to get the muscle to release. Staying in the stretch for longer than 30 seconds and breathing easily into the tight areas will bring results. You're never too old to change your muscle tissue!

Question: Why Is it Hard to Keep Turned Out in 4th Position?

I have a question about turnout. When I go into relevé in fourth or fifth position, it is painful to hold what I consider to be my usual turnout. (I've never had easy turnout; I was born sort of pigeon toed and slept with braces on my feet as a baby.) I guess what I don't know is whether the pain I have while working my turnout is good pain or worrisome pain. How can you tell the difference? How much can you to develop turnout when it's not natural for your hip structure?

Thank you!

April

Let's start with looking at what it means to be pigeon toed. Toddlers under the age of two may be slightly pigeon toed, and yet walk and run easily. The bones of the forefoot sometimes turn inward to create this. Other times the toeing in can be caused by the tibia rotating inward, which is called internal tibial torsion. We have talked about the opposite motion of external tibial torsion in other newsletters. Typically, as the child grows and their muscles develop, the tendency to turn their feet in dissipates with time. Every now and then a more severe case requires some type of casting or special shoes worn when sleeping. It sounds like you had a more severe case, April.

If a child over the age of 3 still has a tendency to walk pigeon toed, they may have an anteverted hip structure. Anteversion is a structural variation at the hip joint where the neck of the femur is angled to create inward rotation of the thighbone. Even with an anteverted hip structure children learn to walk with their feet fairly straight forward by the age of 7 or 8.

It's possible that you have some variation of the above factors, which may make it a little harder to work in a turned out position. The important clue you gave me in your question was that fourth and fifth position is where you felt your discomfort. Even a dancer who didn't have a problem with being pigeon toed as a youngster may complain about holding turnout in fourth and fifth position.

Maintaining turnout is always easier in first and second position. It's when you begin to cross the legs past the centerline of the body that you have problems. The wider the hips a dancer has, the more challenging to hold turnout. A wider-hipped dancer will prefer to stand in an open fourth position and perhaps need to take fifth position with the heel to the base of the big toe on the other foot. Personally, I have always allowed some individual accommodation to my dancers' fourth and fifth, feeling the goal of a plié in those positions was finding center between their two feet and challenging their alignment.

When you go from a stationary fourth or fifth, or from plié, to relevé, the more crossed your starting position is, the harder it will be to hold your turnout. In performance situations, one way I see dancers compensate is by standing primarily on the back leg with less weight into the front leg. There isn't any problem with that compensation unless you have a leg length discrepancy and your longer leg is in front. Then it's harder. A quick note on leg length discrepancies: dancers generally prefer to stand on the longer leg with the shorter leg in front.

My suggestion is to experiment with the amount of crossing in your fourth and fifth positions and see if that helps.

chapter nine

Final Thoughts

One of the major challenges with working with dancers is to help them translate what they are feeling. Is this something that I need to see a doctor about? How long do I work on my own? These are hard questions to answer. Only you know if the way you feel is out of the ordinary, or more than what you would expect from a long hard day dancing.

Let's talk about the difference between soreness and pain.

What Is Pain?

Pain is a complicated process in which our nervous system communicates important information to us. Pain warns us to pay attention to our bodies. It tells us that we are in danger of damaging or hurting ourselves, such as when we get too close to a hot burner on the stove. Pain can be acute or chronic. It is a subjective experience. Acute pain typically gets our immediate attention, like the dancer who comes down from a leap incorrectly and sprains his or her ankle. The dancer KNOWS that the ankle is injured, and the body's response is one of protection—don't even try to walk. Thus, acute pain is easy to define (pain that is extremely sharp or severe). Chronic pain can be more challenging to define and to separate from soreness—especially for dancers, as they appear to have a higher pain tolerance than much of the general population.

When I listen to a dancer describe what he or she is feeling, I remind myself that sensation is relative information. For example, if one has been out in the snow, room temperature tap water will feel hot, but if one has just been out in a hot bath, that same tap water will feel cool. We all have different relationships with our bodies. Some dancers are more acutely aware of small changes and know when something is wrong in their bodies, while other dancers' muscles go into spasm before they notice a change in how they feel.

Improving our ability to listen and respond to messages, such as pain, from our bodies is important to being able to maintain long-term health. It is also important to remember that these responses, which influence how we experience pain, are emotional as well as physical. An example of an emotional influence would be a dancer who is concerned about being taken out of a role. He or she may downplay or deny any pain to keep that role. Looking at the many physical and emotional influences upon pain helps to explain why dancers will have greatly varying responses to the same injury.

There can be a fine line between soreness and pain. More often than not, I see dancers NOT paying attention to their messages of pain or allowing the initial messages of soreness to become pain. Knowing how hard it is to define pain, let's go to the easier task of defining situations that may create soreness.

What Is Soreness?

Dancers often will feel temporary muscle soreness after a class that has been particularly challenging or when new choreography or movement styles have been introduced. This soreness can be caused by overworking the muscles without the proper warm-up for that movement patterning. Combinations in center and across the floor typically use different sequencing and patterns of movements than a barre, modern dance, tap, or jazz warm-up. Depending on your individual body type and structure, some movements will suit you better and feel natural, while other movements challenge your physicality. For example, I am a dancer of normal flexibility and strength. A few years ago I was in a piece that was choreographed by a dancer who was little, wiry, and fast moving. The piece was filled with small, precise, quick movements that weren't a part of my dance vocabulary (think of a robot gone crazy). The day after our first rehearsal I woke up to incredible muscle soreness in my upper body.

Sometimes you will feel soreness begin during a long class or rehearsal. This soreness may be caused by fatigue or doing too many repetitions of a specific movement. If at all possible, when you feel the soreness begin, take a few minutes to rest or stretch the involved area if you have been strongly contracting it. Your body is giving you a clue that if soreness is respected in its early stages, you can prevent more damaging muscle strain.

You may feel muscle strain the day after a class, usually upon awakening. What you are actually feeling are small tears in the muscles and connective tissue caused by overly forceful stretching, movements that you are not accustomed to, or a combination of the two. Generally, you'll feel stiff, achy, and uncomfortable as you begin to move and stretch. Typically these feelings will ease as you continue to wake up and move. It may take a few days for the soreness to decrease, depending on how much you overworked the muscles. For example, if a dancer hasn't danced all summer, and then starts the fall semester by attending a 2-hour modern class followed by a ballet or jazz class, that dancer is bound to feel sore the next day.

Growing Stronger

A muscle grows stronger when it is gently stressed beyond its normal workload. The above example of the dancer taking the summer off and returning immediately to several hours of classes per day describes aggressively overloading of the muscle. This soreness may take several days to disappear, depending on the dancer's quality of body care. The best way to minimize soreness and pain is to maximize training. The following guidelines will help to minimize and work through soreness as quickly as possible:

1. Proper nutrition is essential for the body to repair itself easily and quickly, even from small muscle tears. Protein and good carbohydrates (such as vegetables) should be well represented in the diet. Grains and sweets should be minimized.

2. Proper hydration is important. A general rule for hydration is to drink one quart of water daily for every 50 pounds of body weight. This does not mean soda, juice, coffee, tea, or sports drinks. The body can only utilize about a cup of water an hour, and will flush the rest through the kidneys. Sipping water, all day long, is the best way to stay properly hydrated. Generally, thirst means dehydration.

3. Warm up muscles with movement, such as brisk walking, easy jogging, or marching in place, prior to stretching gently. This approach will help to dissipate any waste products, such as lactic acid, while conditioning the muscles and preparing them for class or rehearsal. It's amazing how many times I see dancers walk into rehearsal without a proper warm-up. Taking class in the morning will not count as a warm-up if your rehearsal isn't until late afternoon.

With practice, dancers will learn to decipher the body's messages as either soreness or pain. Dancers need to know that pain is always a cause for concern and should be respected, especially when trying to determine the pain's origin. Soreness, on the other hand, can be safely addressed through careful attention for a few days. I believe we all have an inner physician, a voice of knowledge, that will give us guidance on deciding what is okay soreness (or good pain as some describe it), and what isn't. We simply need to learn to listen.

My goal is educating dancers to be their own best teachers. When dancers follow the anatomical principles of movement and work within their own physical structure, they are laying the foundation for a long and injury-free career.

On with the dance of life!

Deborah